London's Royal Parks

An Appreciation by
Richard Church

THE
ROYAL
PARKS

Introduction *1*

St. James's Park *7*

The Green Park *13*

Hyde Park *17*

Kensington Gardens *26*

The Regent's Park & Primrose Hill *31*

Greenwich Park *41*

Richmond Park *49*

Bushy Park & Hampton Court *59*

Time Marches On *67*

LONDON : HMSO

Front cover: The Mall, Buckingham Palace's broad processional route, lies within the boundaries of St James's Park

PHOTOGRAPHS: MARTIN JONES

⚜ HMSO

HMSO publications are available from:

HMSO Publications Centre
(Mail, fax and telephone orders only)
PO Box 276, London, SW8 5DT
Telephone orders 071-873 9090
General enquiries 071-873 0011
(queuing system in operation for both numbers)
Fax orders 071-873 8200

HMSO Bookshops
49 High Holborn, London, WC1V 6HB
(counter service only)
071-873 0011 Fax 071-873 8200
258 Broad Street, Birmingham, B1 2HE
021-643 3740 Fax 021-643 6510
33 Wine Street, Bristol, BS1 2BQ
0272 264306 Fax 0272 294515
9-21 Princess Street, Manchester, M60 8AS
061-834 7201 Fax 061-833 0634
16 Arthur Street, Belfast, BT1 4GD
0232 238451 Fax 0232 235401
71 Lothian Road, Edinburgh, EH3 9AZ
031-228 4181 Fax 031-229 2734

HMSO's Accredited Agents
(see Yellow Pages)

and through good booksellers

Printed in the United Kingdom for HMSO
Dd296050 8/93 C50 531/3 12521

A message from David Welch, Chief Executive of The Royal Parks

Richard Church's thoughtful appreciation of the Royal Parks was first published in 1956 but has been out of print since the mid 1970's. It is fitting that it is reissued in 1993, a year that saw the establishment of the Royal Parks Agency dedicated to the enhancement, protection and preservation of the Parks for the benefit of present and future generations.

The intervening years have seen many changes – some of them profound – but the Royal Parks, and the public's affection for them, have survived intact. For this reason I believe that Richard Church's original text deserves to be made available in its entirety. Some of the organisations and administrative structures he mentions have altered or been subject to change but the essential nature of his work is as timeless and pleasing as when it was first penned.

I do hope you will enjoy the book. For our part we will strive to preserve the Royal Parks as refuges from the hurly-burly of city life offering peaceful enjoyment, recreation, entertainment and delight.

David Welch

The Old Police House
Hyde Park
LONDON W2 2UH
071-298-2000

Sunday evening in Greenwich Park

Introduction

*L*ondon, formerly so much abused as the epitome of urban dirt and darkness, the scene of most of Dickens's more dismal nightmares, has gradually changed her appearance, especially during the past twenty-five years. She may be a most venerable lady, two thousand years old, but lately she has had a face-lift, and some of her own children hardly know her. She needs to be reintroduced to them.

This miracle of rejuvenation has been made possible by various sets of circumstances. The only ones which interest us here are those connected with her geographical and historical background. She has been fortunate in possessing, at her very centre, a group of open spaces.

It is true that most of these open spaces have been, and still remain, the property of the reigning Sovereign: but the relations between the Crown and its capital city have always been both intimate and affectionate, surviving even the desperate troubles of the Civil War in the seventeenth century. We know what that relationship means today, and we believe we can see it reflected in the increased freshness and beauty of the Royal Parks, and the happiness which they bring to so many of London's citizens.

This booklet deals only with those Parks which are still the property of the Sovereign. These enclosures (for the word *park* signifies a tract of land, formerly intended for confining beasts of the chase within a wall or fence), by the happy disposition of historical determinants, stretch from the west right into the centre of London at Charing Cross. A visitor could come up from the Kentish countryside on a summer day, walk out of Charing Cross Station, under the Admiralty Arch, and follow the Parks westward almost as far as Shepherd's Bush, his route being along the Mall, round by Buckingham Palace, along Constitution Hill, across Hyde Park Corner into the Park, along the Serpentine to Kensington Gardens, over Holland Walk or through the recently opened Holland Park—not itself a Royal Park—out to the Avenue that leads westward. He might even foster the illusion that he had never landed in London, and that he was taking an uninterrupted rural ride.

That possibility would be due to the long continued benevolence of our reigning Sovereigns, through many centuries of our growth as a people. For our kings and queens have always acted as deterrents toward any predatory persons who have tried to deprive the people of the freedom of the Royal Parks. During the time of the Commonwealth, this freedom was interrupted because much of the Crown land was sold off to speculators, who charged the public an entrance fee. And it must be admitted that Queen Caroline, wife of George II, proposed to enlarge and improve the private part of the grounds in front of Kensington Palace, and to restrict what is now the whole of Kensington Gardens to the use of the Royal Family only. With similar designs upon St. James's Park she asked the Prime Minister, that shrewd country gentleman Sir Robert Walpole, what it would cost to do so? and he drily replied, "Only a Crown, Madam"; an estimate that deterred her.

There may have been some justification for Queen Caroline's desire for greater privacy, because these Royal Parks were originally the environs of Royal homes; St. James's, Greenwich, Richmond, Hampton Court. As we know, some still are the homes, official or private, of the Sovereign and family: some have disappeared, such as Greenwich and Richmond Palaces: others have been added to the Parks in which they still stand, to offer further pleasure to the public.

So much has happened in these Royal Parks that the literature about them is already considerable, and the interested person can consult the books which are listed in the bibliography at the end of this pamphlet. What does emerge is that two kings who have been much maligned by historians with a bias, Charles I and his son the Merry Monarch, were principal in their benevolence in this matter of offering the public access to Crown lands. Henry VIII had made this possible by conserving the southern tract of a great forest, which covered land watered by the Westbourne and Tyburn, two minor tributaries of the Thames, stretched north to Highgate, included "Marybone" (now Regent's Park) and reached south-east into the heart of Westminster. Henry was more interested in hunting than in the amenities of his people; but at that time the problem of breathing space was less acute. In the following sections, as we deal with each Park, the redisposition of this Royal chase will be shown.

Cycling by the Serpentine

As the population of London increased, disproportionately with the enlargement of its consciousness of civic manners, a more formal machinery of control of the Royal Parks became necessary. In 1851 the "duties and powers of management" were handed by the Crown, through Parliament, to the reconstituted Department, the Office of Works and Public Buildings, and the expenses of this management were transferred to public funds voted by Parliament. A series of riots in Hyde Park, which caused much damage in 1866, led to further legislation which has, from time to time, been augmented or amended as occasion has required, and this has been embodied in Regulations brought up to date, at public need, and made accessible to the public through the Stationery Office.

With one exception, the Royal Parks are patrolled by park-keepers, who wear a simple uniform and have the powers, privileges and duties of police constables as well as such extra authority as the Regulations confer. Hyde Park is controlled by the Metropolitan Police, who have a permanent station in the centre of the Park adjoining the office of the Park Superintendent. All this is solely in the public interest, to protect the fabric of the Parks, and to ensure that the fullest possible pleasure may be obtained from them by the greatest possible number of people. In times of emergency, parts of the Royal Parks have had to be closed to the public. I recall that unhappy time in the First World War, when the lake in St. James's Park was drained, and its bed covered with bungalows, to serve as extra offices and a canteen for the overflow of work and staff from Government Departments. And in the later instalment of the World War, Hyde Park was seen to break into a scurf of allotments, camps, anti-aircraft and radar emplacements, and other un-idyllic sores.

These interruptions are but small distresses when we consider how, for nearly four centuries, the majority of the space covered by the Central Parks has been at the service of the public, protected from the gradual tumescence of the town as London spread along and around its boundaries. The amenities have been established, and changed according to horticultural fashion and taste in landscape design, by architects and garden designers whose names have become immortal: Le Nôtre (who planned the grounds of Versailles and so many other great French gardens), Wren, Kent, Nash, to name the most famous. Their genius survives in these groves, swards, ornamental waters, bridges and orangeries.

The public has, on the whole, responded well to its inherited privileges in the Parks, and the machinery for maintenance and protection of the Parks has evolved accordingly in an atmosphere of harmony. The Bailiff of Royal Parks is the head of the Ministry of Public Building and Works' executive parks organization, and his responsibilities are those of a business manager, concerned with general efficiency and co-ordination. The detailed management of each Park is in the hands of a Superintendent; the Central Parks (Hyde Park, Kensington Gardens, St. James's and the Green Parks) are grouped under one Superintendent; Bushy Park and Hampton Court under another. The remaining Royal Parks, Richmond, Greenwich, and Regent's Park with Primrose Hill, each has its own Superintendent. A large staff is required, especially in the Central Parks, where the Superintendent is served by about 300 workers. Forty of these tend the four acres of glass-houses in Hyde Park, where bedding-out plants are raised for the whole group, as well as plants for window-boxes in Government buildings. It will interest the public to know that, at the time this book was first published, the oldest member of that staff was aged 93, the last survivor of the

A famous view of the Whitehall skyline from the bridge in St. James's Park

York Bridge, The Regent's Park
View to the west. King Henry VIII Mound, Richmond Park

gatekeepers known as servants of "The Board of Green Cloth", formerly Royal servants but latterly transferred to Park staff.

The Superintendent's responsibilities are various. He is expected to keep order, maintain the law, design the parterres, raise the seedlings, supervise the trimming, removing and replanting of trees and bushes, protect and encourage bird life on water and on land. A visit, for example, to the world-famous Sunken Garden in front of Kensington Palace, at any time during the positive months of the year, will show how well, and with what inspiration, those duties are carried out. Some idea of the amount of ordering and raising involved is shown by the figures in connection with the flower beds half-surrounding the Queen Victoria Memorial in front of Buckingham Palace. Forty thousand tulips are planted here each year, and these are followed by fourteen thousand geraniums. And a preoccupation with problems of this kind must not allow the Superintendent to forget the need to mow the one-and-a-quarter acres of grass *on the roof* of the Admiralty Citadel, that frowning pile erected at the other end of the Mall during the last war.

On Bank Holidays, and on ceremonial occasions, such as a Coronation, the public are still inclined to leave their litter behind. The Ministry spends at least £14,000 a year of public money in removing it. So serious is this problem that in 1954 the Minister had to set up a Committee to investigate the problem and to recommend methods for combating it. The Report of this Committee is salutary (especially the photograph of the litter strewn by loving subjects in front of Buckingham Palace, the home of the Queen). Amongst the suggestions of the Committee is that of a specially designed and not unsightly litter bin, which we see distributed more copiously about the Parks, to help the public in this matter of civic good manners.

The Royal Parks figure largely in times of national celebration, when stands have to be erected and attention given to the comfort of many thousands of people. In Hyde Park, especially, provision is made for public meetings (at Speakers' Corner by Marble Arch and on the open sward adjoining). On occasions when big crowds attend, such as the May Day celebrations, or political or religious meetings are held, the police control in Hyde Park is carried out with inconspicuous tact and politeness. To steer a gathering of 80,000 people requires an expert technique and an adequate machine. Disturbance of the peace and abuse of the Regulations (especially in the matter of advertising, or collecting of money) are adequately dealt with. Police dogs patrol Hyde Park at night, with attendants, obviously a necessary precaution over so large an area. Twelve policemen are permanently stationed in the Wellington Arch at Hyde Park Corner, beneath the massive forty-ton chariot group called the Quadriga.

It is appropriate that a tour of the Royal Parks of London should begin at Buckingham Palace. Here is the hub, both in fact and in spirit, of these pleasances which we are about to visit. When the Royal Family come out on the balcony of the Palace to acknowledge the loyal greetings of the people, they see to their right hand the length of St. James's Park, with its lake, and the Abbey and Palace of Westminster beyond. So, following the gesture of the Royal right hand, we will enter St. James's, walk round it, and return to the northern end of the Palace and to the Green Park, thus beginning a concentric itinerary which will end in one of the largest, and perhaps the most royal of them all, Hampton Court.

Changing the Guard at Buckingham Palace

St. James's Park
& The Green Park

St. James's Park, which we enter by the gate below the Queen Victoria Memorial, at the corner of Birdcage Walk and opposite the Wellington Barracks, was not always so well-kempt and picturesque as it is today. It was once a swampy flat subject to flooding from the Thames and the Tyburn Stream, the latter flowing through it. It took its name from a hospital for female lepers, called the Sisters of Saint James in the Fields, in the thirteenth century. Henry VIII "acquired" it in 1532, thus making it the oldest of London's Royal Parks. On this enclosure was built the Palace of St. James, which is still the official headquarters of the Crown, as we hear whenever a Royal Proclamation is made. The enclosure was privileged, and the conduct of persons within it severely restricted to conform with the dignity of the Court. Duelling, even the drawing of a sword, was forbidden, and it remained a "sanctuary", though no longer on religious grounds.

The public were introduced to it by the Stuart kings. James I improved and controlled the water supply and set up a menagerie of exotic animals there. Charles I made other minor improvements; but it was his son Charles II who laid it out completely anew, making it as much like Versailles as possible. The swamps and ponds were tidied up, and converted into a long strip of water known as the Canal (after the style of Le Nôtre, the architect of the Park at Versailles). What was then "Duck Island" was preserved by a series of minor channels. King Charles, who loved the place and used to walk freely there, set up a court for the game of *Pell Mell* (a sort of expansive croquet with a touch of the French "boules"), and founded an aviary near what is still called Birdcage Walk. He laid down fresh lawns and planted trees. He then opened his Park to the public.

Improvements were continued during the Hanoverian period, when the Horse Guards Parade was made by cutting off the end of the Canal. George IV had the Park wholly redesigned by John Nash, the Regency architect, on the grand scale. The plan was never fully carried out, unfortunately. Had it been, the Park, the Palace of Carlton House, Regent Street, Portland Place and Regent's Park would have been a unit of distinction. Nash,

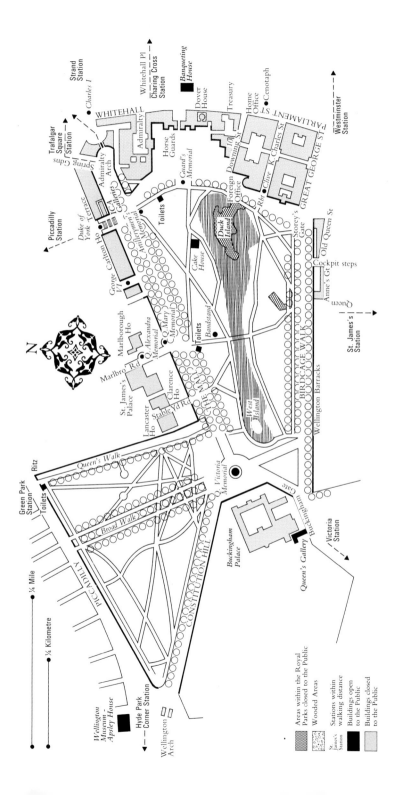

N

Strand
Station

Whitehall Pl
Charing Cross
Station

Banqueting
House

WHITEHALL

Dover
House

Treasury

Home
Office

Cenotaph

Charles I

Admiralty

Admiralty
Arch

Horse
Guards

Downing St

Richmond Terr

K. Charles St

GREAT GEORGE ST

PARLIAMENT ST

Westminster
Station

Trafalgar
Square
Station

Spring Gdns

George Gabion Ho

Duke of
York Terrace

I.C.A.
Galleries

Artillery Mem'l

Guard's
Memorial

Foreign
Office

Duck
Island

Storey's
Gate

Old Queen St

Piccadilly
Station

Toilets

Cake
House

Cockpit steps

Anne's Gt

Queen Anne's Gt

St. James's
Station

Marlborough
Ho

Q. Alexandra
Memorial

Marlbro' Rd

Q. Mary
Memorial

Bandstand

Toilets

St. James's
Palace

Lancaster
Ho

Clarence
Ho

Stable Yd Rd

THE MALL

West
Island

BIRDCAGE WALK

Wellington Barracks

St. James's
Station

Ritz

Queen's Walk

Green Park
Station

Toilets

Broad Walk

Q. Victoria
Memorial

CONSTITUTION HILL

Buckingham
Palace

Buckingham Gate

Victoria
Station

¼ Mile

¼ Kilometre

PICCADILLY

Wellington
Museum–
Apsley House

Hyde Park
Corner Station

Queen's Gallery

Wellington
Arch

■ Areas within the Royal
Parks closed to the Public

Wooded Areas

Stations within
walking distance

■ Buildings open
to the Public

Buildings closed
to the Public

however, succeeded in converting the imitation French lay-out into a wholly English one, changing the Canal into the charming pseudo-natural lake which we appreciate today. Plantations were formed amid a pattern of gravel walks. Thus the Park of St. James took on the appearance, save for a few minor details, which it still retains. The orientation of this charming design was, of course, changed by the removal of the Royal Residence, after Queen Victoria's accession, from Kensington Palace to Buckingham Palace, at that time a somewhat dingy building of badly-weathering Bath stone. The present façade of the Palace was added early in the twentieth century, and now makes an impressive addition to the scene, looking westward from the bridge over the lake.

St. James's Park, being at the heart of the capital, has many historical associations. Charles I was escorted through it from St. James's Palace to Inigo Jones's Banqueting House in Whitehall on the morning of his execution. Not long after, it was the scene of a conversation in which Cromwell said, "What if a man should take upon him to be King?" and received the reply, "I think that remedy would be worse than the disease." Charles II was chided by his brother James for his habit of strolling unattended in the Park. He replied, "They will never kill me to make you King!" The Park has many literary connections, and one might say, without exaggeration, that it served as a back-cloth to the whole of Restoration Comedy, after adding local colour to the diaries of John Evelyn and Samuel Pepys. Dean Swift, in his letters to Stella, wrote in 1711, "This walking is a strange remedy; Mr. Prior walks to make himself fat, and I to bring myself down. We often walk round the Park together." One of those facetious stage pieces was even called *Love in a Wood, or St. James's Park,* too tedious to read now, but useful as giving a picture of the day and night life of high Society when disporting itself in St. James's.

Those Caroline gallants and their ladies added a Watteau-like charm to the scene, but their public conduct would not recommend itself to us today. Violence, as a sport, was indulged in too freely, and we find Swift recording that "I walked in the Park this evening, and came home early to avoid the Mohocks." This was a name given to the "bloods" of the period, who to amuse themselves attacked and even mutilated citizens, slitting their noses, cutting them with knives and swords, upsetting coaches and sedans, and sometimes even causing death. Finally, four of them were caught and tried at the Old Bailey, and they were fined three shillings and four-pence! Such conduct was not envisaged by Henry VIII when he first fenced in the Park, and thereby "devised and ordained many and singular commodious things, pleasures, and other necessaries, most apt and convenient to appertain only to so noble a prince, for his singular comfort, pastime, and solace." Nor would John Milton, that mighty poet and great servant of the State, have approved had he still been living in his official residence, the garden house in Petty France, overlooking the Park.

Uncomfortable things continued to happen right through the eighteenth century, and in 1804 two sentries swore on oath that while on guard at the Recruit House (now Wellington Barracks), "I perceived the figure of a woman without a head, rise from the earth at the distance of about two feet before me, I distinctly observed that the figure was dressed in a red striped gown, with red spots between each stripe, and that part of the dress and figure appeared to me to be enveloped in a cloud. In about the space of two minutes, whilst my eyes were fixed on the object, it vanished from my sight." However, in the celebrations of 1814, to mark a Royal Jubilee and the suspension of the war with France, the vast crowds in St. James's Park were comparatively orderly, even when the display of fireworks got out of hand and set alight the tall Chinese pagoda which was consumed with the loss of several lives.

We are more docile even than that today. All that remains to make our conduct exemplary on public occasions and in public places, is to put our litter in the handsome bins freely distributed about the Parks.

The walk round the lake is delightful: one of the most popular promenades in London. The scenes from the middle of the bridge over the lake, west to Buckingham Palace, east to the Horse Guards Parade (with the fairytown skyline), must cheer many a jaded office worker during lunch-hour, while visitors from farther afield linger there, enfilading the prospect with batteries of cameras. The weeping willows, with their hanging fringes carefully trimmed, add an almost Chinese touch to the scene, and this exotic effect is heightened by the presence of the now famous

Pelicans have been an attraction in the park since the seventeenth century

pelicans, and ornamental ducks, whose family origins can be studied in the identification tiles displayed under glass on the north bank of the lake, near the refreshment kiosk. The abundance of wild birds in all the Royal Parks can be appreciated by the help of the series of booklets on "Bird Life in the Royal Parks." This is too vast a subject to deal with here, but W. H. Hudson, the naturalist, who was also a master of English prose, had much to say about it in his *Birds in London.*

Duck Island is a breeding-place and sanctuary, unfortunately somewhat over-patronized by the hordes of starlings who flock in nightly to roost in Central London. The six pelicans at present on the lake are all Eastern Whites, presented by the late Amir of Bahawalpur. Two were presented in 1966, three in 1963 and "Paul", the largest, in 1957. A smaller bird, "Daphne", who lives alone in the Pelican Pool on Duck Island, is an American White presented by the Governor of Louisiana in 1957. She met with an accident in 1963, and her damaged wing had to be amputated. At 4 p.m. the pelicans parade on the lawn near the old Birdkeeper's Lodge (on Duck Island) to receive their ration of fish. Spectators will also observe the notice-board, pleading with the public not to feed the pelicans with odd scraps, which endanger their lives.

Wild duck of various kinds, such as mallard, tufted duck and pochard, nest on Duck Island. In addition, over twenty species of duck and geese have been introduced from all parts of the world, divertingly dressed in their national costumes. Black-headed gulls come up the Thames and are to be seen in the Park for most of the year. Many have been "ringed" in St. James's, to be found long afterwards in Germany, Sweden, Denmark and Finland.

But a mere catalogue of flora and fauna does small justice to the unique character of St. James's Park. The dignity of the Mall, the finest boulevard in London, with Nash's Carlton House Terrace, and the several Palaces on the right, with the Park on the left hand, serves to frame (with Birdcage Walk) the seeming wildness and insouciance of the scene. The charm is indescribable in words. It has an Eastern touch, as of a willow-pattern plate. Yet it is English too, with nostalgic references at every turn and in every monument; naïve and fresh even in its sophistication, because age has mellowed its artifices, already sufficiently draped by nature.

We need, of course, to make several circuits of St. James's before leaving it for the Green Park. We must keep to the lake-side first, then take the outer walks down Birdcage Walk, along the Horse Guards Parade, and up the Mall. Finally, to see the flower-beds, which with those of Hampton Court are the finest in Town, we need to explore the labyrinth of paths which criss-cross the Park. The annual show of dahlias, inside the gate opposite Cockpit Steps in Birdcage Walk, has the opulence of a painting by Rubens, or our contemporary Sir Matthew Smith.

Feeding birds against an historic skyline

*T*he **Green Park** is quite different in character. It has no flowers, except for a flush of bulbs along the short slope beside Piccadilly, near the Ritz Hotel. It accords well with its name, for it is heavily wooded and the ground is well watered (although the Tyburn, which once crossed it, is now confined within sewer-pipes). The grass always has a lush, dark verdancy, reminiscent of the grounds round the châteaux of the Loire in France, rather than of English lawns. The trees too are luxuriant, their heavy foliage hanging nearly to the ground, so that one walks there with one's personality reduced to "a green thought in a green shade." It is a restful process for tired nerves.

Entering the Green Park from the Mall, behind the Queen Victoria Memorial, we find ourselves at the end of the Queen's Walk, named so after Caroline, wife of George II. She had this walk prepared in 1730 so that the Royal Family might there "divert themselves in the spring." It stretches alongside the green undulations, seemingly half-sunk, with the great houses of the exclusive village of St. James on its right hand. It ends at the Ritz and Piccadilly. On its south side Constitution Hill divides it from the grounds of Buckingham Palace, and offers a shaded drive between the Queen Victoria Memorial and Hyde Park Corner. A description of this "hill" in 1750 is amusing; "a pleasing ascent to one of the finest eminences in nature, commanding a vast extent of variegated country bounded by distant hills." Those hills would be the alpine heights of Wimbledon!

Before Charles II added these acres to the Royal Parks, the ground was meadow land, where duels were fought. Sir Thomas Wyatt, with his Kentish army on Hay Hill (at the top of Berkeley Street), fought an artillery battle with Queen Mary's troops (at what is now Hyde Park Corner) in the rebellion of 1554, a protest against her marriage to Philip II of Spain. During the Civil War the Roundheads fortified this "finest eminence in nature" with a redoubt and battery.

Charles II, a man of peace, used Green Park for more pleasurable purposes. He built there "a snow-house and an ice-house, as the mode is in some parts of France and Italy, and other hot countries, for to cool wines and other drinks for the summer season." Charles's democratic habit of strolling among his subjects is said to have given the name to the hill where he so frequently took a "constitutional", valuable not only for his health, but as a pointer toward the development of the unique nature of our monarchy.

The Wellington Arch, at the top of the hill, was designed by Decimus Burton the architect, in conjunction with the monumental entrance to Hyde Park at Hyde Park Corner. Against his advice, a huge statue of Wellington was set up on the Arch, but this was removed in 1883 and re-erected at Aldershot. It was replaced by the present chariot group by Adrian Jones. Each leg of the Arch contains three storeys, partly taken up by the police station already referred to.

For so peaceably intended a spot as Constitution Hill, several inappropriate incidents have occurred there. An attempt was made to murder Queen Victoria, and a revolver was cast before King Edward VIII.

The Green Park, like Kensington Gardens, has its "Broad Walk." This is really part of the design for the Queen Victoria Memorial, from which it runs, between a grove of trees, up to Piccadilly. There are ornamental iron gates at each end, those by the Memorial being given by the Dominions. Those at the top formerly stood at the entrance of Devonshire House (by the corner of Berkeley Street opposite their present site), and were erected to conclude the grove in 1921, making a handsome addition to the general design of the view down to the Memorial and the Palace. The Park ends at Hyde Park Corner, having served as a handsome link in the green chain stretching westward, and as a garden to Mayfair.

Green Park provides a peaceful haven

The Constance Fund Fountain

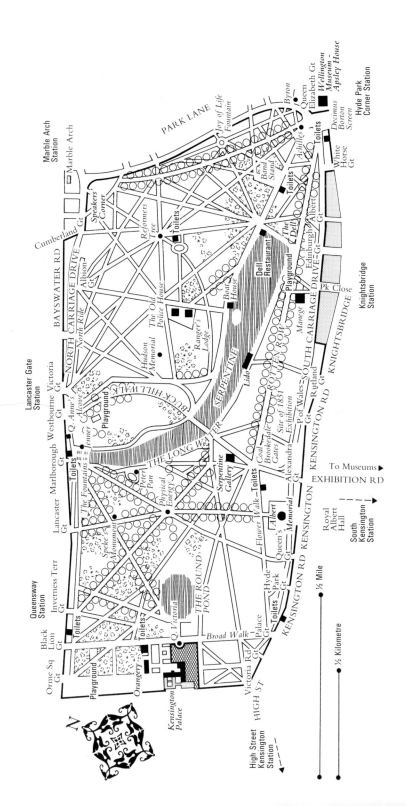

Hyde Park

*H*yde Park was formerly the large, central part of the forest which Henry VIII reserved for hunting. Its area today is 340 acres, while Kensington Gardens, which adjoin it, cover 275 acres. A stranger may find it difficult to locate the boundary between the two Parks, for the natural division would seem to be the northward curve of the long stretch of water consisting of the Serpentine and the Long Water. The division actually runs from Alexandra Gate in Kensington Gore, over the Serpentine Bridge (designed in 1826 by Rennie, the architect of the old Waterloo Bridge) and along Buck Hill Walk to Victoria Gate in the north, on the Bayswater Road.

Indistinguishably joined, the two Parks are different in character, though it is not easy to define that difference. But Speakers' Corner, at the extreme north-east corner of Hyde Park, needs only to be contrasted with the Sunken Garden in the precincts of Kensington Palace at the farther end of Kensington Gardens, for the contrast to be appreciated. The two spots are two miles apart. They are also two centuries apart. Speakers' Corner, and its overflow across the open green south-westward toward the Superintendent's Lodge and the Serpentine, are a hub of human activity and excitement, not only because of the public debates held there on every day of the year, but also because they receive the crowds surging down from Edgware Road and westward from Oxford Street, the latter probably the busiest thoroughfare in London, the great artery dividing north and south, and opening east and west. Richard le Gallienne, the Edwardian poet, walking exhausted into the Park at this point one hot summer day, sat down near Speakers' Corner and wrote some verses for the evening paper which employed him. They ended:

> So I found me a fane for my weary feet,
> And a pen, and a pipe, and a pot,
> And I made me a ballad of Oxford Street;
> And why the devil not ?

There is no reason why he should not; but he might have been more happily employed on a ballad about the open spaces of Hyde Park, which are the most characteristic feature of the place.

Long before Henry VIII's reign, the manor of Eia was the official estate of the Master of the Horse. Away back to the time of the making of Domesday Book, this tract of forest had been a thickly planted and populated region; but the plants were primaeval trees, and the haunt was not one of orators and holidaymakers, but of deer, boars and wild bulls. For centuries it was part of the estate of St. Peter, Westminster, but in 1536, that year of economic as well as religious revolution in England, it became the property of the Crown; and so it has remained. Queen Elizabeth I valued it as a Royal hunting ground, but she also introduced the practice of holding military reviews there. The hunting has long ceased, but the military manoeuvres and ceremonies are still held there on special occasions.

James I opened Hyde Park to the public, and during his son's reign it became a popular resort. Here foot and horse races were held, some under Royal patronage, morris dances were performed, and refreshments sold, including "milk from a red‑cow." This practice of dispensing milk direct from the cow continued until the nineteenth century.

Under the Commonwealth the eastern side of the Park included some of the fortifications erected to defend the city against the Cavaliers from the west. A large square fort with four bastions was built near what is now Hyde Park Corner, and close to the site of the present Marble Arch stood a strong-point where the credentials of travellers from the west were examined, and their persons searched for dispatches. Cromwell and his staff reviewed their troops in the Park.

After the triumph of the Roundheads, the Royal Parks were confiscated and thrown open more fully to public use, only to be sold into the hands of speculators three years later. The Parks, however, were included in the Restoration, and their amenities once more fully appreciated by the public, who were able to resume their play of an early form of football, called "hurling matches", which combined our now national winter game with all-in wrestling.

In this park was a large enclosure called The Tour (and afterwards, The Ring), a circular drive where courtiers and their families (as well as others than their families) drove round daily in equipages on which was lavished vast wealth. The brilliance of this spectacle is recorded in the diaries of both John Evelyn and Samuel Pepys. On May Day, 1663, Mr. Pepys decided that it might be officially advantageous if he were to take part in the fashion parade round The Tour, where he hoped to be noticed by the King and the powerful Lady Castlemaine. He dressed for the occasion in new clothes, at considerable expense, with "painted gloves", very pretty and all the mode", and he records that Mrs. Pepys said he "looked mighty noble." He rode his own "dull jade" from his home in the City to Charing Cross, where at the Chequer Inn he

This memorial to Queen Caroline was unveiled by Her Majesty Queen Elizabeth II in 1981

changed his mount for a lively horse. There he overstepped himself, for this spirited animal, after carrying him safely to the scene of ostentation, got out of hand, and Mr. Pepys had to retreat without being seen by the King and the ladies of the Court.

Charles II restocked the Park with deer, but confined them to the enclosure called Buckdean Hill, now Buck Hill, the area between the North Ride (by the Bayswater Road) and the Superintendent's Lodge, in the middle of the Park.

At that time, and into the reign of William and Mary, the Park ran as far as Kensington, and a house called Nottingham House. King William, however, removed the Court to this house, converting the premises into a Palace. The long and rural journey from the new Court to the City and Westminster offered highwaymen and footpads a rich beat, and William III had the road between St. James's and Kensington Palace lit with three hundred oil lamps. During the summer the lamps were stored in the woodyard at the Palace. This is the first instance of any road in England being illuminated at night. The installation was not wholly successful, for the robberies continued, and we hear of Horace Walpole, fifty years later in 1749 while returning home from Holland House, having his carriage stopped in Hyde Park by two highwaymen, who presented a blunderbuss and relieved Walpole of his gold watch and eight guineas, a large sum at that time.

Such unlawful practices are not wholly suppressed, and even today the Park has to be patrolled at night with trained police dogs, which were introduced into the staff of the police station in the Park as a means of stopping the snatching of ladies' handbags. The presence of the dogs reduced this particular little game from a harvest of 235 handbags to 18 in 1954. This precaution, and the technique for dealing with the huge crowds that congregate on special occasions, have already been mentioned.

The greatest of these occasions was the Exhibition of 1851, when the Crystal Palace, designed by Paxton, was erected in the Park on the site just westward of the cavalry barracks at Knightsbridge, facing Rutland Gate. So much has been recorded of that triumph of Empire, that it need not be further commented on here. The only innovation since then, to command so much controversy, has been the setting up of the Lido by George

Contrasting moods in Hyde Park

The Italian Gardens and the Peter Pan statue by the Long Water in Kensington Gardens

Rowing boats beside the Serpentine Lido

Lansbury in 1930. Formerly, swimming in the Serpentine was allowed only in the early morning, and it was restricted to males. George Lansbury's paternal touch, while First Commissioner of Works, altered all that. Now men, women and children can bathe from 6 a.m. until dusk in the summer. A charge is made to enter the enclosure and light refreshments may be bought in the pavilion. When the weather is attractive, many thousands of swimmers and sunbathers enjoy the Lido every day.

What gives Hyde Park its distinction is the stretch of water known as the Serpentine. The Park was formerly watered by the Westbourne, a minor tributary of the Thames, which flowed from Hampstead. This stream, with a contribution of several springs in the Park area (some of them said to be medicinal, and others supplying Westminster Abbey with water; see the Memorial Pillar at the east end of the lake, where the Abbey Conduit House once stood), was used for creating the lake in 1730, a small one which filled what is now called the Dell, the most picturesque spot in Hyde Park, where moorhens and ducks may be seen. The Westbourne, however, proved to be both unruly and more and more contaminated with sewage as London grew. After much experiment, the cleansing of the Long Water and the Serpentine was begun in 1869, a layer of putrid mud fifteen feet thick being removed. The stream was confined in pipes and carried direct to the Thames, while the lake was supplied by storm water and surface drainage, with extra supplies pumped from the well on Duck Island in St. James's Park when needed. The Round Pond in Kensington Gardens is fed from the Serpentine. The island in the Serpentine is artificial, created as a bird sanctuary. The bridge built by Rennie in 1826-8 marks the boundary between the Park and the Gardens, and also between the Long Water and the Serpentine.

Many people are curious about the Standing Stone in the Dell. Though it has a druidical appearance, and though there is a

The Achilles Statue near Hyde Park Corner

legend that it was brought to its present site by King Charles I from Stonehenge, its history is in fact much shorter. It is a piece of Cornish stone that formed part of a drinking fountain erected in 1861 and subsequently removed. This stone, weighing seven tons, was left on the site.

From the time Hyde Park was first opened to the public, it has been the fashionable arena for horse-riders. The increasing cost of this sport, and the changing tastes of the people who could afford it, have greatly thinned the morning parade of mounts along Rotten Row. Before the World Wars, most social figures, male and female, of Mayfair and St. James's, were to be seen taking their noble exercise in the Park, while their grooms congregated at the several gates, waiting to lead the horses back to stable.

Rotten Row is the parade everyone has heard of, and it deserves its fame, for the prospect of it, leading westward from Apsley House (now the Wellington Museum), is a stately scene, especially on a sunny day in summer, when the golden medallions of fire from the sun tumble through the foliage of the plane trees and elms, subdued with dustmotes to form an ancient but still regal currency. The Row dips and rises again, adding to the viewer's prospect of the riders, who move flickeringly through the beams and shadows, like figures in a dream of heraldry.

Rotten Row, with its extension, the New Ride, is $1\frac{1}{2}$ miles long. The horseman can continue round the North Ride (2 miles long) which includes "the Ladies' Mile" on the north side of the Serpentine. More adventurous riders can cross Hyde Park Corner to the horse-tracks along Constitution Hill and the Mall. The most open ride in the Royal Parks is the five-mile track in Richmond Park.

Boating has been permitted on the Serpentine and the Long Water since 1847. Skating during winter is restricted according to the thickness of the ice, which must be not less than five inches. Fishing in Hyde Park is permitted only between the Lido and the east corner of the Serpentine. Not much provision for children's games has been possible in Hyde Park, but there are football pitches along the south side, where the Great Exhibition was held.

Hyde Park has a number of monuments and drinking fountains, many of them the gifts of private donors during the past century and a half. One of these is the Achilles Statue, by R. Westmacott, R.A., erected in 1822 to commemorate the victories of Wellington, and commandingly placed on the strip of land between the park boundary and the southern end of the Broad Walk. It is a modified copy of one of the horse-tamers on the Quirinal at Rome, and was cast from cannon captured at Salamanca, Vittoria, Toulouse and Waterloo. Prudish English aesthetic taste was shocked by the nudity of the male figure. One complainant, writing to *The Morning Herald*, said that if his mother "who was a Newcastle woman, had caught any of her children looking at such an object, she would have soundly whipped them." The balance between morals and propriety has shifted its fulcrum since then.

Another gift to Hyde Park is a fountain which bears the title Joy of Life. It was given by the Constance Fund, an organization founded in 1944 by the late Mrs. Constance Goetze in memory of her husband, who died in 1939. This fountain stands on the Park Lane side of the Park, and it may be of interest to know that nearly four tons of bronze were used for casting the figures.

Marble Arch, now outside the Park, formerly stood at the entrance to Buckingham Palace. It was adapted by Nash, that architect of superb taste, from the famous arch of Constantine in Rome. It is built of Carrara marble, and the ornamentation is by Flaxman, Westmeath and Rossi. The Arch was moved to its present site in 1851. Like the Wellington Arch at Hyde Park Corner, it is able to house a posse of police. The gate is opened only for the passage of Royalty.

Before the realignment of roads as a result of the Park Lane Improvement Scheme, at the junction between Oxford Street and Edgware Road in front of the Arch, a triangular stone in the roadway marked the site of the famous Tyburn tree. Here public executions were staged, on a massive equilateral triangle of poles about twelve feet high, each of the three sides offering space for eight victims. The turnpike was last adorned with this macabre spectacle in 1783. Military executions and floggings were carried out nearby. It is ironically appropriate that Speakers' Corner should adjoin these sites, to emphasize how our British social consciousness has emerged toward more civil articulation, with freedom of opinion and speech, which may be demonstrated here, by citizens of any degree of eccentricity or fervour, so long as their eloquence shall not be obscene, blasphemous, or an incitement to a breach of the peace.

In the secluded hollow just north of the Serpentine, near the buildings of the police, the Ranger's Lodge, and the Superintendent's office, is a bird sanctuary, marked by a bas-relief monument, a memorial to W. H. Hudson, the naturalist and prose-artist. Jacob Epstein carved the figure of Rima surrounded by a formalized flight of birds (a figure taken from Hudson's romance *Green Mansions*). The unveiling of this monument by the Prime Minister in 1925 provoked bouts of philistinism, and the bas-relief was defaced several times by green paint. Since then Epstein's genius has created a new orthodoxy and a world-wide public.

North of the bird sanctuary is the nursery, where, in four acres of glass-houses, the bedding-out plants for the Central Parks are reared. Farther to the west, facing the lake, is the Cockpit, a shallow amphitheatre, where oratory may be indulged. Buildings nearby known as the Magazine were once a military depot. Beyond this we cross the handsome bridge designed by Rennie to enter Kensington Gardens.

The Dell restaurant

Kensington Gardens

*W*e enter **Kensington Gardens** by Mount Gate, from the south side of the Serpentine Bridge. Not far away, on the edge of Hyde Park, we will observe a new building, a restaurant of contemporary design, where we might like to replenish ourselves if we have walked right through Hyde Park. Resuming our way, we follow the Flower Walk westward on the south side of the Gardens, walking parallel with Kensington Gore, and passing, on our left hand, the Albert Memorial and the Albert Hall. The former has been cleaned, and its wartime derangements repaired, so that its elaborate collection of sculptured allegories can be fully appreciated.

The Flower Walk is a delight at all times of the year. Like the Sunken Garden toward which we are walking, it is a sheltered bosquet, whose combination of ornamental trees and flower-beds is thoughtfully planned for every month, almost every week, of the floral year. And there is usually a friendly gardener at work with whom one can chat about the disposition of the perennials and bedded-out plants. These two features of Kensington Gardens are certainly as beautiful as any horticultural display in Europe. Bird life, so prolific and so various here, seems to have been little affected by the cutting down of the great but decaying trees of nearby Broad Walk. I have seen tree-creepers, spotted flycatchers, and even a great spotted woodpecker, flitting among the trees in the Gardens, and during one windy March afternoon I watched a jackdaw swaying in the branches, or fans, of the cedar near the approach to the Albert Memorial.

The Flower Walk ends at the beginning of the famous Broad Walk, by Palace Gate. Until 1953 this wide promenade, rising past Kensington Palace northward to Black Lion Gate in the Bayswater Road, was flanked by an avenue of ancient trees, most of them elm, planted by George II's Queen Caroline when Kensington Gardens were laid out. Much controversy and public criticism was roused when these veterans were cut down, as being a danger to users of the Gardens. Following this conservative agitation, the Minister of Works appointed in 1954 a Standing Advisory Committee to assist the Department in its control over

The statue of Physical Energy was erected in June 1904

the planting, pruning, felling and preservation of trees throughout the Royal Parks. The public may be assured that the supervision by this committee of specialists in arboriculture, with the vigilance of the park-keepers, will continue to protect the safety of visitors and the scenic character of the Parks. It is to be hoped that when the gaps are filled, attention will be given to the legend that the elms were originally planted according to the disposition of the Guards at the Battle of Blenheim.

Nothing is more sobering than the death of an ancient tree, as so many of our English poets have observed; but trees are mortal, and have their day, and their diseases. They can also, like human beings, be replaced. The Broad Walk has already been replanted with limes and Norway maples. They are a welcome substitute for the elms, for limes flourish in the London air, and the perfume of their bloom in July is as nostalgic as that of a field of beans, or a hedgerow fugal with honeysuckle. It brings to mind, through the senses, the very essence of all countryside life, and of an impossible Golden Age. So the first Report by the Advisory Committee on Forestry resulted in a good work which nobody is likely to dispute, and which our grandchildren will endorse with still greater pleasure .

Beyond the Broad Walk, facing east along the middle of Kensington Gardens through the broad avenue to the Long Water, stands the Palace which William III made his home, and where he established the Court in 1689. The original Gardens in front of the Palace consisted of twenty-six acres taken from Hyde Park. Queen Anne added further Gardens from the same source, and additions made in the reigns of George I and George II brought Kensington Gardens to the size they are today. It was Queen Caroline, wife of George II, who caused the formation of the Serpentine and the Long Water by damming the Westbourne, but her intention of annexing large areas of Hyde Park for a new Palace was never realized. The lay-out of the Gardens was much more formal than that of Hyde Park, and this was appropriate to the surroundings of the Palace. Three avenues converge on the Palace, on much the same plan as those which lead to Hampton Court Palace. The boundary between Hyde Park and the Gardens was formerly a sunk fence (or ha-ha), but this was later filled in and railings substituted, inside which wheeled traffic is still prohibited.

The surroundings of the Palace are varied in their beauty. Passing the statue of Queen Victoria, which was made by her daughter H.R.H. Princess Louise, Marchioness of Lorne, we turn left along a path toward the Palace, and at once come upon the famous Sunken Garden, again on our left hand. It is surrounded by a walk closed within pleached lime trees, through which are cut, at intervals, squints into the garden, and openings for ornamental iron gates. It is impossible to describe the Garden. It lies, an emblem of quietude, colourful for most of the year, formal in shape, with a rectangular pond along the centre, containing three leaden tanks. The flower beds are herbaceous, and perhaps one may say that the most opulent scene there is in August; though personal taste in colour schemes will have to decide on this matter. The noble trees loom up round the Garden, giving it an air of secrecy, in spite of its squint holes through which the public may overlook its meditation. The Palace, which Sir Christopher Wren enlarged, adds the signature of a great artist to the beauty of the Garden. Between the trees can be seen snatches of the walls, roof, and chimney stacks of the noble yet modest building where Queen Victoria was born in 1819 and where she received news of her accession in 1837.

To the north of the Sunken Garden, set back across a formal green planted with clipped bay trees, stands the Orangery, designed in 1704. It now contains a series of classical statues and casts of the kind favoured in the eighteenth century, when the Orangery was thronged with bewigged figures in flowered suits, moving to the sound of music by Lully, Vivaldi, or Doctor John Bull. Seats inside the building offer winter shelter to visitors, where they can dream of summer and look across the lawn to the corner of the Palace, and imagine themselves back in that time. Further to conjure the mood of historical pleasure, the visitor can walk a few yards to the Palace where the State Apartments are now open to the public. The east part of the Palace houses the London Museum, a collection of treasures associated with the story of London for over two thousand years, and formerly displayed in Lancaster House.

The rear precincts of the Palace are still almost rural, and can be seen from Palace Green, where the novelist Thackeray lived in his later years. Wren House, and an adjoining row of small cottages, will interest connoisseurs of domestic architecture.

The view from the east front of the Palace, right through Kensington toward London, is majestic. It remains as a monument to a way of life that has vanished along with the sedan chair, the harpsichord and the three-cornered hat. The great trees, standing like galleons, so that one half expects them to move together, as a fleet, over the sea of lawns, are so disposed about the landscape that glimpses are offered, here and there, of further and further reaches of parkland, fading into the London air, whose half tangible fumes reduce the brightness of the green, so that it becomes almost unreal, a canvas by an old master of landscape painting, a John Crome or a Peter de Wint, its quality more than "half as old as time."

Near the top of Broad Walk, to the left, is the Children's Playground, a feature found in most of the Royal Parks. The swings there were given by J. M. Barrie, creator of *Peter Pan*, whose fairy personality is celebrated in a statue by Sir George Frampton which stands beside the Long Water (on the western shore). The Elfin Oak, at the end of the Playground, is a venerable stump brought from Richmond Park. An artist, Ivor Innes, was commissioned to work on the natural forms—bosses, holes, indentations—to increase their suggestions of animal shapes. A world of small creatures, beloved by children, has thus emerged from the gnomic sculpturing of nature, together with elves and pixies. The Elfin Oak has been renovated by the comedian, Spike Milligan.

The North Walk, inside the Bayswater Road fence, leads to the top of the Long Water and the fountains. Two springs formerly flowed here, one called St. Agnes's Well, for drinking water, the other medicinal, of euphrasian property, a cure for sore eyes. The present building nearby, called the Pumping Station, is said to have been designed by the Prince Consort in imitation of the Petit Trianon at Versailles. It is now a loggia, and a pleasing addition to the formal waters and potted plants at the head of the Long Water.

If we follow the shore of the Long Water, on the right hand, passing the Peter Pan statue, we can, at will, turn into the heart of the Gardens, by footpaths that converge to a junction in the centre where stands the statue of Physical Energy, by G. F. Watts, a bronze cast of the original which forms the centre of the Cecil Rhodes Memorial on Table Mountain at Cape Town.

We can approach the Round Pond along any of these paths, and watch the exciting sport of model-boat sailing, similar to the activities that take place around the edges of the pond in the Luxembourg Gardens in Paris, though there the cries of enthusiastic owners are in a different language. As the Round Pond is also a bird sanctuary, high-powered model speed boats (in minature) are forbidden. The public, as well as the birds, benefits from this restraint. Without preservation from the noise and the stench of machinery, the Parks would no longer be sanctuaries, where human beings and birds can commune with each other through the language that was spoken, and sung, in the Garden of Eden; a haunt in which we can still imagine ourselves to be lingering, on a spring or summer morning, under the shadow of the great trees in Kensington Gardens.

The Magazine

The Regent's Park &
Primrose Hill

T he **Regent's Park and Primrose Hill,** like Hyde Park
and Kensington Gardens, were originally part of the great
chase or hunting forest, appropriated by Henry VIII in the
sixteenth century. This wide tract of wooded pasture-land known
as Marylebone Park Fields was so named after the parish church of
Tybourne Village, which was dedicated to *St. Mary at the Bourne.*
This name is a reminder today that Regent's Park is well watered,
though the famous and historical stream is no longer visible, being
confined in conduits on its journey to the Thames. It rose in the
Hampstead heights, and flowed down to the Thames which it
joined at three places, one at Grosvenor Road, Pimlico, the other
two at Westminster, below the Abbey. Thus the Tyburn River
has determined much of the character of three of the Royal Parks:
Regent's, the Green Park and St. James's, whose artificial waters
have been formed through the subjection of this stream which
formerly had such sinister association with the gallows, the Tyburn
Gibbet at Marble Arch.

"Marybone Park" remained a royal hunting demesne until
1646, when Charles I granted it to two of his supporters as security
for debts incurred by him during the Civil War. The
Commonwealth Government seized the Park, along with all
Crown property, and sold the timber and deer to pay similar debts.
It reserved 3,000 trees for naval construction. At the Restoration
the Crown resumed possession, but did not reopen this land to the
public. Instead, the King let it to various noblemen.

Visitors to Regent's Park will instantly be impressed by the
handsome and stylistic frame in which the Park is set. This
surround of terrace houses was part of an ambitious design by the
Prince Regent in 1811, when the last lease, to the Dukes of
Portland, expired. He planned to build a Palace in the centre of
the land and to connect the Park with Carlton House by the
newly laid out Regent Street. This noble extravagance was never
fully realized, but it was carried far enough to leave for posterity a
whole district of urban domestic architecture of great dignity.

The first amenity to be enjoyed in Regent's Park today is
not its trees and verdure, but the terraces which surround it. Since

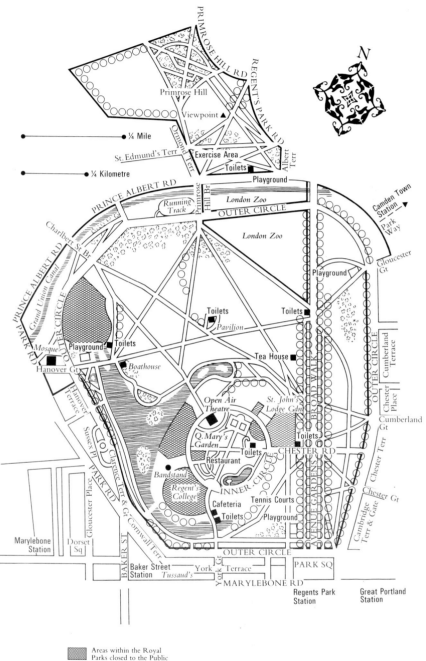

N

¼ Mile

¼ Kilometre

PRIMROSE HILL RD

REGENT'S PARK RD

Primrose Hill

Viewpoint ▲

St. Edmund's Terr

Ormond Terr

Exercise Area

Toilets

Albert Terr

Playground

PRINCE ALBERT RD

Primrose Hill Br

London Zoo

OUTER CIRCLE

Camden Town Station ▲

Park Way

Running Track

London Zoo

Charlbert St. Br

Gloucester Gt

Playground

OUTER CIRCLE

Grand Union Canal

INNER CIRCLE

Toilets

Toilets

Cumberland Terrace

Pavilion

Playground

Toilets

Tea House

Broad Walk

Chester Place

Mosque

PRINCE ALBERT RD

PARK RD

Hanover Gt

Boathouse

Hanover Terrace

Cumberland Gt

Cumberland Terrace

Open Air Theatre

St. John's Lodge Gdn

Chester Terr

Sussex Pl

Clarence Terr & Gt

Cornwall Terr

Q. Mary's Garden

Toilets

Toilets

CHESTER RD

Chester Gt

Restaurant

Bandstand

Regent's College

INNER CIRCLE

AVENUE GARDENS

Cambridge Terr & Gate

Cafeteria

Toilets

Tennis Courts

Playground

Gloucester Place

Marylebone Station

Dorset Sq

BAKER ST.

Baker Street Station

Tussaud's

OUTER CIRCLE

York Terrace

York Gt

PARK SQ

OUTER CIRCLE

MARYLEBONE RD

Regents Park Station

Great Portland Station

Areas within the Royal Parks closed to the Public

Wooded Areas

St. James's Station Stations within walking distance

Buildings open to the Public

Buildings closed to the Public

the repair of wartime dilapidations, these terraces dominate the scene with renewed charm and grace. Several gates into the Park interrupt the continuity of the terraces, each being given a name of contemporary interest at the beginning of the nineteenth century. Clarence Gate, by which we enter as we come up from Baker Street on our way from Kensington Gardens, was sited to please the great actress Mrs. Siddons, who lived at the top of Upper Baker Street overlooking the Park. She implored the Prince Regent not to block out her view with his new terraces. He, being a prince of some culture with a respect for the arts and their practitioners, complied by setting Clarence Gate so that Mrs. Siddons could retain her view into the Park.

There have been many famous people who have lived in the terraces, among them Mrs. Fitzherbert, wife of the Prince Regent, and Macready the actor, who was a friend of Browning the poet, who is said to have proposed to Miss Barrett under an oak tree in the Park near York Gate. The painter J. M. W. Turner lived for a while in one of the terraces, as also did his namesake, the poet and critic W. J. Turner, who died in 1946 in a house in Sussex Place, near Clarence Gate. Charles Dickens once lived nearby at 1 Devonshire Terrace (opposite the Royal Academy of Music in Marylebone Road), and he used the Park freely to air his large family.

The design of the terraces, Regent Street, and the lay-out of the Park were by John Nash, at that time the official Architect and Surveyor of Woods and Forests. Nash had a great sense of style, though in designing the pavilion at Brighton for his Royal patron he was forced, by the Prince's taste for the fashionable Oriental, to desert his own Palladian restraint. His neo-classical façades in Regent's Park, however, gave a new character to the Park, which had formerly been completely rural, with farms and cottages, the only regal accent being in the old manor-house, a five-gabled Tudor mansion, used as a hunting lodge by Queen Elizabeth I. Here, in 1600, she entertained the Emperor of Russia and his suite. The house, which stood facing the present York Gate, on a site near the Devonshire Mews, was pulled down in 1791.

The several enclosures in the Park, one of which is the Zoological Gardens, were formerly in private hands, or let to

Sussex Place designed by John Nash

societies. The lease held by the Royal Botanic Society was not renewed when it lapsed in 1932, and the use of ground in the Inner Circle of the Park by the Royal Toxophilite Society (for the preservation of the sport of archery) has also been discontinued. Present policy is to absorb these enclosures, thus adding to the availability of the 472 acres comprising the Park as a whole. An example of this welcome addition to the Park is the retreat called St. John's Garden, attached to one of the villas of the Inner Circle. This formal enclosure, within its walls of pleached limes, has a privacy which I am reluctant to dispel by undue advertisement. The view of the house from the closed end of the Garden, through a vista of high hedges and flowerbeds, has something of the withdrawn charm of the Petit Trianon.

Adjoining this delightful Garden is St. Dunstan's, famous during the inter-war period for the work it did for the blind. It was so badly damaged by enemy action, however, that accommodation for the blind has been obtained elsewhere.

Among the few remaining enclosures within the Park are Bedford College and its annexe to the north. The college, for women, is part of London University. It stands in its own grounds (including a well-stocked flower-garden) between York and Clarence Gates, backing on to the Inner Circle.

The Inner Circle is part of John Nash's original design for the lay-out of the Park, of which this exactly circular road to the east of the two arms of the lake was the hub. The lake and the Inner Circle may be likened to the balance of a gigantic watch, as can be seen from the map. The outer road is circular only in theory, for it runs in straight stretches beneath the shadow of the several Regency terraces framing the Park, and cutting into it for only a short distance to the north, where it runs through the Zoological Gardens and alongside the Regent's Canal. From Park Square (which is not within the Park) at the south-east corner, the Broad Walk runs straight to an entrance of the Zoological Gardens, and crosses the canal by a foot-bridge. It is really a continuation of Portland Place and Regent Street, and is thus an integral part of the great design that never fully matured. The flower-garden, along this impressive avenue, was laid out at the wish of the Prince Consort. Several Victorian garden ornaments survive, and the two large flower-vases are still filled each season with hundreds of plants.

The Dolphin fountain, originally in Hyde Park, now replaces the Swan drinking fountain, a dilapidated, dry and ugly piece of statuary which failed to complete the character of its surroundings.

The open ground between the Outer Circle and the canal, to the north-west of the Park, is the principal sports area, and includes a well-marked running track. This reminds us that Regent's Park caters lavishly for school-games and adult sports: football, cricket, tennis, golf instruction, hockey, lacrosse, netball, archery, athletics, and rowing and sailing on the lake.

The lake, so picturesque with its arms and several islands, was made between 1796 and 1833, by damming the waters of the Tyburn, which crossed the Park on its way down to Westminster and the Thames. Two small tributaries, both rising from springs in the Park or nearby, joined it here, the confluence flowing along the low-lying ground east of Winfield House, the residence of the United States Ambassador. One of these contributions to the Tyburn Stream rose in swampy ground now included in the Zoological Gardens. From the Park, the stream crossed the Outer Circle road at Upper Baker Street, followed the course of Marylebone Lane, crossed Piccadilly into the Green Park, where it divided into a main stream and a mill-stream, the latter running down to Millbank, where it once fed the mill maintained by the

Abbey of Westminster. The main stream subdivided just behind the Abbey, to embrace a patch of flat ground called Thorney Island, on which the Abbey now stands. Such monastic sites are usual throughout the country, clean water and rich pasture being necessary accompaniments to civilization.

The Regent's Canal is a short waterway. It was opened for traffic in 1820, when this means of transport was being generally developed, to be almost immediately superseded by the railways, which came two decades later. The making of this canal, which runs from Paddington to Limehouse, where it joins the Thames, caused the upper waters of the Tyburn to be cut off. This ended a long riparian story, for the little river was the first to be utilized, in the Middle Ages, as a means of water supply for London, conduits for this purpose being built in the thirteenth century. Both the lake and the canal have been the scene of fatal accidents. In 1874 five barges loaded with explosives were being towed along the canal, and while passing under the Macclesfield Bridge (in the N.W. corner of the Park) one of them blew up. The bridge, the Superintendent's House and pay house were wrecked, and three people killed. A disaster on the lake occurred on 15th January 1867, when the ice gave way beneath a large crowd of skaters. Forty people were drowned. The lake was afterwards drained and the bottom levelled at a depth of $4\frac{1}{2}$ feet.

The Outer and Inner Circle are joined by many paths, and one can approach the most intimate heart and beauty of the Park from all points. Within the Inner Garden lie the Open Air Theatre, and Queen Mary's Garden, where there is one of the fullest and best planned roseries in the country. It was begun in 1932, with a gift of bushes from the British Rose Growers' Association, through the Empire Marketing Board. Further gifts from the same source, in 1933 and 1949, filled these widespread beds to capacity, creating so regal a result that King George V, even before the final gift, approved the suggestion that the Garden should be named as *Queen Mary's*. In the Garden is a small lake with an island built up as a rock-garden, lavishly furnished with alpines and miniature perennials, and round which one may walk, like Gulliver in the land of Lilliput, charmed by diminution; the tiny dianthus, phlox and other miniature alpines and rock plants are a delight to the specialist and a wonder to the casual passer-by.

Top and bottom left: Queen Mary's Rose garden and the Children's boating pool, The Regent's Park

A panoramic view of London from the top of Primrose Hill

Greenwich Park: The London skyline and Canary Wharf from the Wolfe statue

The Flower Garden in spring

The formal splendour of York Gate

Queen Mary's Garden contains also a wide sweep herbaceous border, which replaces a former border that butted out somewhat incongruously with the general plan of the gardens. The new border not only disguises an old disused water reservoir, but consorts with the green barrier at the opposite side of the garden, behind which lies the Open Air Theatre. This arena was opened in 1932, and the enterprise has since fought bravely with the caprices of our climate. Shakespeare's plays are most popularly given, though opera and ballet have been performed from time to time. It can seat an audience of 4,000, and has a marquee for refreshments before and after each performance.

To the west of Queen Mary's Garden is a fountain in black marble by Sir William Reid Dick, R.A. It represents a boy studying a frog. This fountain was given in 1936 by the late Sigismund Goetze, a generous benefactor of the Royal Parks, to whose memory there stands at the head of the Garden a handsome fountain group in bronze, set in a stone basin. This group, by William McMillan, was erected in 1950, and presented by the Constance Fund.

All that survives from the Royal Botanical Gardens is the group of fossil tree trunks posed beside the lake. A legend in front of them tells their story.

Visitors will be impressed by the quietness of Regent's Park. This character may account for the wide variety of bird life to be found there. Some twenty species of ducks, ten species of geese, and a pair of black swans have been introduced in recent years, inhabiting the lake and its six islands, while herons and kingfishers are sometimes seen. Willow warblers and whitethroats have bred in the Park, and goldfinches also nest there.

Primrose Hill has its own charm

After the variety and picturesqueness of Regent's Park, Primrose Hill may appear comparatively desolate. Its name suggests what it must have been like in the past, when it was a southern-sloping elevation overlooking farmland, and the distant prospect of pre-industrial London. A southern slope catches the first warmth of spring-time sunshine; that is why Primrose Hill undoubtedly lived up to its name in the past, and even today has something of that vernal promise about it, so that one climbs to its summit in a mood of exhilaration, eager to gaze out from that height (206 feet) over the panorama of London, whose roofs and spires have now reached and surrounded it. There was until recently a "panorama" set on a stand at the top of the Hill, to point out the features of the urban landscape, as far as the Surrey and Kentish hills south of London. But unfortunately this index was made of soft metal, and could not withstand the attention of hooligans, who appear to have made Primrose Hill one of their last retreats against the rising tide of general education. A second "panorama" was mounted on the Hill, so that the public could identify individual features of the distant London scene, such as St. Paul's, the Abbey, the Victoria Tower at Westminster; but this shared a similar fate, and has been removed.

The slopes of the Hill are still semi-rural, with stretches of grass and groups of hawthorn and other trees. Near the foot of the Hill stands Shakespeare's Oak, planted in 1964 to mark the four hundredth anniversary of Shakespeare's birthday. Its predecessor was planted in 1864 by the Victorian actor Samuel Phelps; and Eliza Cook, at that time a distinguished poetess who lived at Peckham, wrote an ode for the occasion. Unfortunately that tree died in 1958 and had to be replaced.

This effort to give the Hill cultural respectability appears to have been only partially successful, as we have seen. But Primrose Hill has had a long history of disorderliness, and at least one mystery story. It was before Sir Edmund Berry Godfrey, J.P. for Westminster, that Titus Oates made his first depositions on oath. Subsequently Oates swore that Godfrey complained of affronts from the Privy Council to which information on the depositions had been laid. Godfrey is reported to have become apprehensive, but declined advice to go about with a servant for protection. On 17th October 1678, his dead body was found in a ditch on the south side of Primrose Hill, "face downwards, transfixed with own sword"; his pocket book and cravat were missing, but his valuables untouched. Evidence was given at the inquest that he had been strangled and then stabbed after death; the verdict was wilful murder.

In the atmosphere of the Popish plot, this event created a panic. Three men were convicted and hanged at Tyburn in connection with the murder, though there was never any evidence on the motive or the identity of the criminals, which remains to this day a mystery.

From the time that the forest oaks were cleared away in Elizabeth I's reign, Primrose Hill appears to have been a place for public demonstrations, and quickly gained a reputation for rowdiness. Duellists resorted there, and the military used it for maneouvres. Such large-scale destructive processes, however, ceased in 1842, when the Crown acquired the Hill from Eton College, fenced it in, provided a gymnasium, made paths and lighted them with gas-lamps. In 1902 the old pond on the north-western side of the Hill was filled in, and twenty acres of reclaimed ground laid out for football and cricket. The only duel of any note fought here was in 1821, that between Scott, Editor of the *London*

Magazine, and a perfectly innocent man named Christie. Christie had been tricked into the fight by his dastardly principal, Lockhart, the son-in-law of Sir Walter Scott, and contributor to the Edinburgh paper *Blackwood's Magazine*, in whose columns he had advised the English poet John Keats to "go back to his gallipots" as an apothecary's assistant, and to give up the effort to become an immortal.

Even the slopes of Parnassus are subject to hooliganism, and therefore Primrose Hill, a very minor foothill to that mountain, need not be unduly condemned. The only other literary associations are through the private houses at the base of the Hill. In one of these Lady Bryon died in 1860. In another lived Hepworth Dixon, editor of *The Athenaum*, an influential literary journal in the nineteenth century, which was merged with other weeklies in the nineteen-twenties. In a third house lived the distinguished writer on child psychology, Susan Isaacs.

Primrose Hill has been doleful in its historians as well as in its history. In the twelfth century it was described as being "full of the lairs and coverts of beasts and game, stags, bucks, boars and wild bulls", and as late as 1778 it was approached "by way of deep and dirty lanes." In that same century Mother Shipton prophesied that "when London surrounds Primrose Hill the streets of the Metropolis will run with blood." In spite of these dire associations, the Hill remains open to the south and the first influence of spring. It still gives a noble prospect of almost the whole of London, and offers a momentary retreat to her citizens.

Stone tazza in Regent's Park

Greenwich Park

People who are inclined to associate **Greenwich Park** with the somewhat dreary approaches from Central London will be surprised when they discover this highly individual place, a beauty-spot in its own right, deserving a fame other than that which it has possessed as the determinant of the degrees of longitude. "Greenwich Mean Time" is known all over the world. The tiny hill, south-east of London, shaded with massive sweet chestnut trees, overlooking the Thames and the vast expanse of London, across a classical foreground created by Wren and Inigo Jones, is less universally known.

Historically, it is the oldest of the parklands included in our survey, for though as a "Royal" Park it is not so old as St. James's, it is certainly the oldest of the fenced domains, being thus enclosed by Humphrey, Duke of Gloucester, in 1433. James I replaced the fence by a wall in 1619. The period between those two centuries was one of Royal splendour at Greenwich, for the Palace was Queen Elizabeth's favourite home. The Park, with the adjoining Blackheath, however, has a still older history, as its name shows; *Greenwich* being a word of Saxon origin, meaning the "green village." Its site must always have attracted settlers, for here was a place above the river mists, convenient for shipping, not too far from the growing centre of London, while being in itself peaceful, healthy (a gravel soil) and superbly situated with views east, north and west. The Romans, experts in picking good sites, chose this one. It is probable that they drove their famous London to Dover road, or at least a diversion from that road, through Greenwich Park, along the valley which we can still follow just below the Observatory, and above the Queen's House, which now forms part of the National Maritime Museum. It is not known what buildings the Romans put on the site, for much human traffic has trodden there through the centuries. Relics of a Roman villa have been found on the slope above the valley, consisting of a patch of tessellated pavement, some nails and coins, and fragments of Samian pottery.

The Romans were not the first to appreciate this prominent site. Twenty-five "barrows" or tumuli, on the south-west corner of

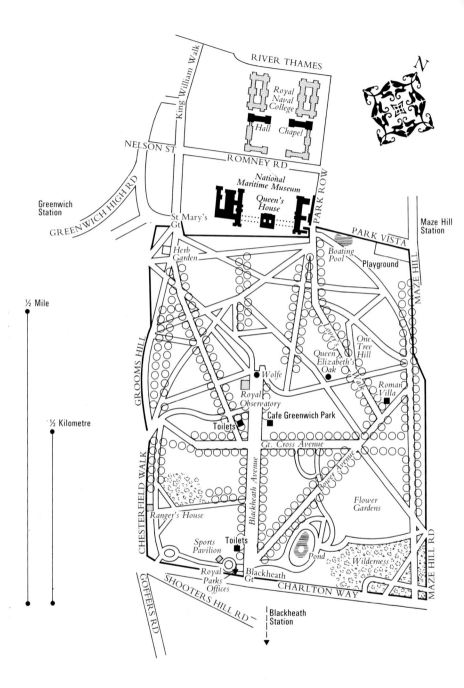

RIVER THAMES

Royal Naval College

Hall *Chapel*

King William Walk

NELSON ST

ROMNEY RD

PARK ROW

National Maritime Museum

Queen's House

Greenwich Station

GREENWICH HIGH RD

St Mary's Gt

PARK VISTA

Maze Hill Station

MAZE HILL

Herb Garden

Boating Pool

Playground

½ Mile

GROOMS HILL

Lover's Walk

One Tree Hill

Queen Elizabeth's Oak

● *Wolfe*

Royal Observatory

Roman Villa

½ Kilometre

Cafe Greenwich Park

■ *Toilets*

Gt. Cross Avenue

Bower Avenue

Flower Gardens

CHESTERFIELD WALK

Blackheath Avenue

Ranger's House

Sports Pavilion

■ Toilets

Pond

Wilderness

MAZE HILL RD

Royal Parks Offices

Blackheath Gt

CHARLTON WAY

GOFFERS RD

SHOOTERS HILL RD

▼ Blackheath Station

N

Areas within the Royal Parks closed to the Public

Wooded Areas

St. James's Station — Stations within walking distance

Buildings open to the Public

Buildings closed to the Public

the Park, near the Crooms Hill Gate, have still to be fully identified, but it is most probable that they preceded the Roman occupation, and are of Bronze Age origin, though legend has attributed them to the Danes, who were encamped on Blackheath in 1011.

The mediaeval Duke of Gloucester built a castle on the highest part of the Park. Henry VIII greatly enlarged this grim fortress, and it continued to play a part in Royal domestic life until Charles II demolished it in 1675 to make way for the Royal Observatory, built by Sir Christopher Wren. The Duke of Gloucester also built a Palace by the riverside, which he named *Placentia,* and here Henry VIII, the Queens Mary and Elizabeth his daughters, were born, and here his son Edward VI died. The Queen's House behind it (a handsome example of the work of Inigo Jones) was built by Charles I for his wife Henrietta Maria. It lies at the foot of the slope as we look down from the Observatory approach, and the end of the well-posed Blackheath Avenue. This avenue leads from the heath to the Observatory and is closed by the statue of General Wolfe, the hero of the Battle of Quebec (1759). Wolfe lived at Macartney House, neighbouring White House outside Crooms Hill Gate.

Charles II, perhaps hating the Palace which had been appropriated and lived in by Cromwell, pulled it down and began building a new one, but only one block designed by John Webb was completed. William and Mary made the Palace over for a hospital for seamen and new buildings were designed by Wren. The magnificent grouping of the Hospital buildings creates the foreground of the view from the Observatory. The scene is unique, the classical buildings lying at the foot of the slope, with the River Thames beyond, so emphatic in their authority that we forget the slums on each side, and see only a landscape that might have been painted by Claude or Poussin (except for the two power stations at Greenwich and Deptford whose discharge has made astronomical observation impossible, so that the Royal Observatory has had to remove itself to Sussex). This picture of the Hospital, with the river approaches to London westward and the Thames Estuary to the north and east, is so impressive that it dominates the whole character of Greenwich Park. The casual visitor will remember it first when recalling the pleasures of the

A famous view of Greenwich Park and the Royal Naval College

place; and so must the habituee, who has had opportunities of studying the panorama under all conditions of light, at all seasons of the year. It is a painter's task, rather than a poet's, to describe the most revealing view of London obtainable anywhere around the encircling height of the vast city.

All this, however, is accessory to, rather than part of the Park, which we can now turn to, after being baffled by that view as one is always baffled when confronted with perfection, in life or in art.

The Observatory buildings, now abandoned by scientists for Hurstmonceaux, are being divided into those of merit sufficient to be shown to the public, and those to be demolished. All the historic buildings are being retained and opened to the public as part of the National Maritime Museum. One of these, Flamsteed House, is already on view to Park visitors. The Observatory has had a great record, and has brought many famous men to Greenwich Park, among them the philosopher-mathematician Isaac Newton, described by Wordsworth as

Voyaging through strange seas of thought, alone.

One of the domes in the Observatory has been converted into the Caird Planetarium, where people can see the heavenly patterns, in miniature, made by the working of the force of gravity, surely a suitable tribute to Newton.

The savage Russian Emperor, Peter the Great, seeking civilization, came to England for a while, and rented John Evelyn's home in Deptford, where he played havoc by riding his coach (?)

between Evelyn's wide yew hedges. Evelyn, the diarist and friend of the other diarist, Samuel Pepys, was a pioneer in landscape gardening. They both mention visits to the Park. So did Boswell many decades later, though he records that Dr. Johnson, while praising the beauty of the Park, considered that "it did not equal Fleet Street."

Outside the Observatory are set a barometer and a plate made of compensated metal giving the standard measures of length. By following the path through the gate round the north wall of the Observatory, the visitor may see the Meridian Stone, which marks the zero degree of longitude stretching due north and south. From this the longitudinal measurements are marked all around the world.

Having examined these relics of the world of mathematics, and having exhausted our imagination in the effort to comprehend the full significance of the view over the Hospital buildings below and London beyond, we return along Blackheath Avenue to the gate on to the heath. The view back along the avenue is worth a moment's pause, for General Wolfe stands up against the sky, his face turned toward Quebec in Canada, and he makes a clear-cut and decisive figure in contrast with the soft contours of the trees bordering the avenue. We turn in left, and cross the Ranger's Field, a perfect example of an English village green, surrounded by old trees and commanded by the Georgian garden-façade of the Ranger's House. The field is now a cricket ground, and no more appropriate setting could be found.

The house, once dilapidated and forsaken, now belongs to the London County Council and has been sumptuously restored. It used to be the residence of Queen Caroline when she was Ranger of the Park. Later, it was the home of the Lord Chesterfield who was so vigorously castigated by Dr.Johnson in the Preface to his Dictionary, following the Earl's refusal to be a patron to the work. Chesterfield had written a book also, consisting of a series of *Letters to his Son*, inculcating an elaborate and artificial system of European manners. Johnson said of this book that it taught "the manners of a dancing master and the morals of a whore," a characteristic example of the forcefulness of Johnson's literary criticism. It also shows how to bite the hand that has refused to feed you.

Returning to the Blackheath Gate, and passing to the left of the Superintendent's House, we turn off through a gate from the Bower Avenue, into the approach to the flower-garden. This forms a large triangle on the eastern end of the Park, with the greenhouses and the Wilderness to its right. The Wilderness is rightly named, being an enclosure of thirteen acres, with a carpet of bracken and wild flowers. It is also a bird sanctuary, and in the more open parts a herd of some twenty fallow deer is kept.

The Gardens are most impressive because of the ancient sweet chestnut trees, whose huge trunks are particularly decorative, with whorled indentations patterning the bark. Many fine cedar trees stand on the lawns, their sombre fans offering a happy contrast to the blaze of the flower-beds. The small lake, with an island, has been given a cement bed, but this has been done so that the natural effect is not spoiled; and that is consonant with the whole character of Greenwich Park, which, in spite of the setting amid so densely populated a congeries of industrial and maritime suburbs, is emphatically that of a country estate at any time in the seventeenth or eighteenth centuries.

The water of the lake still laps at grass edges, with clumps of water-plant to break the line. From the tiny island cascades fall into the lake, keeping the water on the move and thus aerating it. Views from several points around the lake show the imaginative skill with which the water-garden has been planned. The weeping willows with their pale lamentation of drooping fronds, the flowering shrubs and prunus, the magnolias and catalpas with their pallid leaves, all by their freshness contrasting with the deeper green of the native timber, are so harmonious together that one forgets that this colour symphony is not the unconscious artistry of nature. Passing on, however, toward the flower-garden proper, and admiring the variety of magnolias on the way, one quickly appreciates the human skill which maintains the rose-beds, the herbaceous borders, and particularly the dahlia border, running along the north-eastern boundary of the flower-garden. This border, seen at the end of August, is a triumphant blaze of colour, stretching between Vanbrugh Park and Maze Hill Gates. As a further signature of gaiety to the scene, there stands a bed of begonias near Vanbrugh Park Gate, a solid block of delicate pink punctuated with silver-grey plants of *Eucalyptus globulus*. I hesitate,

Flamsteed House

however, to specify beds of flowers, for they are almost as elusive as the expressions that cross the human face. Every season sees changes in a formal garden; but it is improbable that visitors will see anything incongruous in the flower-beds of Greenwich Park, or indeed in any of the Royal Parks.

Beyond the flower-garden, and turning north-west along Lovers' Walk, we pass the site of the Roman villa on our right, and see the Magnetic Observatory on our left. There is a touch of wildness again in this part of the Park, as we take a right-hand footpath to climb One Tree Hill. This is now populated by many more than one tree, but it still offers a good view westward across south London and the hills of Sydenham and Denmark Hill. On the latter we can see the heavy tower of the Salvation Army Training College. This hardly compensates for the loss of the Crystal Palace, that crowned Sydenham Hill until the disastrous fire destroyed it in 1936, thus removing not only a loved landmark, but also a chapter from the history of Hyde Park.

Reaching Park Row Gate, at the end of the Queen's House, we turn right to the children's quarter, which fills the north-eastern extremity of the Park. The playing ground, with sand-pit and a wealth of swings, see-saws and other semi-gymnastic toys, together with a boating pond, is the largest of all those in the Royal Parks, as it needs to be, for beyond the wall in front of it lies a district of labyrinthine streets.

Walking back westward along the northern boundary of the Park, we find another well-tended bed of flowers in the sunk garden that was formerly the ha-ha separating the Park from the grounds of the Queen's House. Reaching the main gate of St. Mary's, we turn back eastward again along the valley below the Observatory, until we come to an old relic called Queen

Elizabeth's Oak. It is now a tall stump some twenty feet high, cloaked in ivy, and railed to prevent further damage being done to it. The stump is hollow, and legend says that at one time the tree was used as a lock-up for offenders against the Park Rules. This tree, under which legend also says that Henry VIII once danced with Anne Boleyn, is a survivor from the forest that formed part of Blackheath, an outriding of the vast Forest of Anderida that stretched right across south-east England through the Weald, working its way up through the breaks in the North Downs, the range to which Greenwich plateau and Shooter's Hill are an approach. Tree-planting went on in the Park systematically through the seventeenth and eighteenth centuries. John Evelyn, a pioneer in arboriculture, whose estate covered the whole of what is now Deptford, may have been advisory in this matter when Charles II was busily engaged in transforming the Palace and grounds of Greenwich. The Spanish chestnuts were planted in 1665, the year of the Great Plague, and the French architect Le Nôtre was consulted about this.

Over a thousand elms, in addition to the avenues of Spanish chestnut, were planted at that time, as well as sixteen small coppices of birch, hawthorn, ash and privet. The hawthorn, so attractive a tree either as hedgerow or standing out alone on grassland, is still a prominent feature of the Park, adding to its spring-time gaiety. Queen Elizabeth's oak, twenty feet in girth, with a hollow interior six feet across, died in the eighteen-seventies. Some of the living chestnuts are as large, and as we know many of them to be over two centuries old, it is an impressive speculation to guess the age of the historical oak that died nearly a century ago. We might, too, conjure to its now mortuary shade the ghosts of mortals who have stood beneath it, ordinary folk, "pale kings and princes too", through the ages, perhaps among them the poet and spy, Christopher Marlowe, who was done to death in the near neighbourhood of the Park in 1593 when all hereabouts was seething with Court activities, and the anxious traffic which always surrounds the seat of a Government. All that has subsided, and Greenwich Palace, with its Park, is now a peaceful retreat. But it still overlooks the centre of the British Commonwealth, at Meridian Zero, and holds its awe-inspiring place between the Eastern and Western hemispheres.

Richmond Park

The very sound of the names, **Richmond** and **Hampton Court,** creates a holiday mood, and an escape from the smoke and rumble of London, which the seclusion and charm of the inner Royal Parks cannot quite evade. Richmond Park has an area of some 2,470 acres, and is $2\frac{1}{2}$ miles across from north to south and east to west. With its heights, its great stretches of bracken, its plantations (most of which are now thrown open to the public), its Royal lodge and the noble avenue called Queen's Ride, it offers still the illusion of the great days of the feudal estates. Even the motor cars on the roads encircling the Park (which should be left in one of the nine car parks, and not by the roadside or on the grass verges) cannot spoil the character of the place: the solitude, the atmosphere of old England, the spacious dignity. One could well spend a summer holiday by making daily excursions to Richmond Park, exploring on foot, with a map, and one of the several guide-books and W. H. Hudson's evocative essay *A Hind in Richmond Park.* I would recommend also, for this quiet holiday, a copy of *The Seasons*, whose somewhat formal blank verse was written in 1727-1730 by the Scottish poet, the indolent James Thomson, while he lived on the edge of the Park overlooking the famous view across the Thames (near the Richmond Gate and the *Star and Garter*).

Every season of the year can be enjoyed in Richmond Park, for here is wild nature aided rather than restrained, and landscape as virgin as it was when the land was first enclosed in 1637 by Charles I, to enlarge the original grounds of Richmond Palace. The Palace stood between the Thames and Richmond Green. Charles wanted to extend the range of his hunting, and, not without opposition from owners of land adjoining East Sheen, he walled in the great area which, in 1649, the Commonwealth Government expressly excepted from the general sale of Crown lands. It was given to the City of London as an act of favour, in return for the support given during the Civil War. At the Restoration, the Corporation of London returned the Park to Charles II "by way of restitution and not of gift", an act which the tactful and witty King recognized as a gesture "not of restoration,

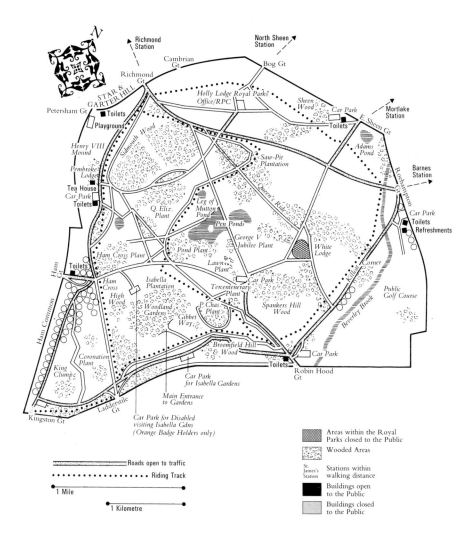

Richmond Station

North Sheen Station

Cambrian Gt

Bog Gt

Richmond Gt

Holly Lodge Royal Parks Office/RPC

Sheen Wood

Car Park

Mortlake Station

E. Sheen Gt

STAR & GARTER HILL

Petersham Gt

Toilets

Playground

Sidmouth Wood

Toilets

Henry VIII Mound

Adams Pond

Barnes Station

Pembroke Lodge

Saw-Pit Plantation

Tea House

Car Park

Toilets

Roehampton

Q. Eliz. Plant

Leg of Mutton Pond

Queen's Ride

Car Park

Toilets

Refreshments

Pen Ponds

George V Jubilee Plant

White Lodge

Ham Cross Plant

Pond Plant

Lawn Plant

Killed Corner

Ham Gt

Toilets

Isabella Plantation

Tercentenary Plant

Spankers Hill Wood

Public Golf Course

Ham Cross High Wood

Woodland Gardens

P. Chas. Plant

Beverley Brook

Gibbet Way

Coronation Plant

Broomfield Hill & Wood

Car Park

King Clump

Toilets

Robin Hood Gt

Car Park for Isabella Gardens

Ham Common

Ladderstile Gt

Main Entrance to Gardens

Kingston Gt

Car Park for Disabled visiting Isabella Gdns (Orange Badge Holders only)

Areas within the Royal Parks closed to the Public

Wooded Areas

St. James's Station — Stations within walking distance

Buildings open to the Public

Buildings closed to the Public

═══════ Roads open to traffic

•••••••••••• Riding Track

1 Mile

1 Kilometre

but of a free gift." He and his successors continued to use the Park as a hunting ground.

During the eighteenth century it was somewhat neglected, but Sir Robert Walpole and his son (the latter being Ranger at that time) set about to improve it. They also restricted public entry, a course of action furthered by George II's daughter Princess Amelia, who became Ranger in 1751. Her restrictions led to a lawsuit, sponsored by a liberty-loving brewer named John Lewis, whose persistence won the case, and maintained a right of way for pedestrians. Lewis chose a ladder rather than a gate (which might be locked against the public), and this shrewd decision is still commemorated in the name of Ladderstile Gate, by which the Park is entered from Kingston Hill.

Let us, however, enter the Park by another gate—there are six for carriages and ten for pedestrians. Coming to the Park from over Wimbledon Common and Putney Vale, we cross the Beverley Brook (which runs through the eastern quarter of the Park) and turn in at Robin Hood Gate. The aspect of the Park from this entrance is characteristic. It rises up slowly to the horizon, a stretch of open country broken by a thick spinney (Spankers Hill Wood) ahead, and Prince Charles Spinney to the left. The middle of three roads passes through the gap, toward the distant view across the centre of the Park, and round by Pen Ponds, the two artificial lakes made in the eighteenth century from the stream that ran through the Park. These are preserved for fishing enthusiasts, and consequently bathing is not permitted.

The Pen Ponds abound in fish: pike, bream, carp, roach and eels. Perch, dace, gudgeon and tench have also been taken. Scattered about the Park are some twenty-five smaller ponds, mostly old gravel pits. Now they serve as watering-places for the deer. Adam's Pond, at the extreme north of the Park, by Sheen Gate, is reserved for model-boat sailing (motor boats are forbidden to avoid pollution of the water, as deer drink here). During the last war the Pen Ponds had to be drained because they formed a landmark for aircraft. The opportunity was taken to clean them before refilling. They are a picturesque asset to the Park, as may well be seen from the road in front of White Lodge, whence they lie to the left of the Queen's Ride, shining against the afternoon sun. The gentle slope toward them, graduated open country punctuated with ancient oaks, is a favourite haunt of the red and fallow deer, who pass and re-pass, through the bracken, under the trees, and out into the open, half real, half fabulous.

Perhaps the most famous features of the Park are the deer and the old oak trees. The fallow deer are the smaller, dapple creatures. Their herd is over 350 strong. Its males are called bucks, its females does, and its youngsters fawns. The red, or Scottish deer are large, and their males, the stags, are magnificent animals, reigning over a herd of 250. The females are called hinds, and the young, calves. The two kinds do not interbreed, because their rutting seasons are a month apart. The females of both kinds wander away from the herd when their time is come to calve, choosing a lair in the bracken, or the beds of nettles expressly left to grow for that purpose. A few days after the birth, they rejoin the herd with their infants. The males live amiably together in the herds until the rutting season begins. During the spring their antlers drop off, and new ones form, covered in velvet. As the rutting disturbance looms, the males become restless, and rub their antlers violently against the trunks of trees, sometimes drawing blood in the effort to remove the velvet and to prepare for battle. The season arrives in autumn and lasts for about six weeks. During that time the stags roar and fight with each other. It is wiser not to approach them while this selective contest is in progress, though there is no need to fear them. Dogs, however, should be kept under control at this time, and also when the females are running their young. One blow from the hoof of a hind or a doe will break the back of the biggest dog.

The deer range freely all through the year, but in winter they are given additional food, in the large pens constructed so that the young can slip inside and eat from the bins at the same time as the stags, who are kept outside the pens. In snowy weather, it is a great sight to see the herds gather to follow the waggon carrying food to the pens, at 2 to 2.30 p.m.

Royal Warrants still obtain, by which certain officers of the Government and Crown receive haunches of venison twice a year. The two Archbishops, and members of the Cabinet, are included in this ceremonial distribution. The remainder of the kill is marketed to help pay the cost of upkeep of the herds.

The gamekeeper can tell us about less conspicuous wild life in Richmond Park. There are, for example, two badger setts (large burrows), each containing a "boar" and "sow" and family. The badger is a very clean animal, and is useful in consuming wasps' nests and bumble bees' nests. They are shy creatures, and seldom seen, their public appearances being made mostly in autumn, the mating time. They litter in February, "at the last peck of the robin", as the gamekeeper said, a phrase which reveals how arcadian life in Richmond Park can be.

Maytime in the Isabella Plantation, Richmond Park

Bushy Park, deer grazing safely
Donkeys Corner Pond

Horse riding near Ham Gate

In so large a sanctuary, of course, wild life is various and abundant. Hares dance in March on the open ground, and an occasional fox follows their movements with interest. Rabbits have almost disappeared since the scythe of myxomatosis swept the country. The grey squirrel, that vermin, preys everywhere in the park, especially in the wooded enclosures, and weasels are common.

There are no rooks in Richmond Park, although crows, jackdaws, jays and magpies are present. The largest enclosure in the park, Sidmouth Wood, just inside Richmond Gate, used to be the nesting ground of herons, but unfortunately none can be found there today. The highest spot in the Park is King Henry VIII Mount, made for that monarch to take his stand during the great drives of game when the hunt was on.

Though there is no more hunting, other sports are provided in the Park. There are five cricket pitches, two golf courses, and twenty-four football grounds. Riding is allowed all over the park up to 1 p.m. weekdays and 11 a.m. weekends and bank holidays, except when the going is soft, when riding is confined to the riding tracks and roads.

The staff required to maintain all this huge estate is of course in short supply today, and the public need to be the more-cooperative in consequence. There are 31 keepers, including two motor-cyclists, one with a Land Rover, and three mounted on horses, and eighty industrial workers. In spite of this shortage, common to all branches of the agricultural and horticultural worlds, the Superintendent here, like his colleagues in all the other Royal Parks, has contrived since the war to develop many further amenities, to clear away old eyesores, and to plant new Gardens.

The outstanding innovation in Richmond Park is the opening of the Isabella Plantation to the public. Formerly it was a thicket almost impassable with timber and an undergrowth of rhododendrons. A tiny, rippling stream has now been diverted through it, with glades leading off, and plantings skilfully set to give surprise vistas. The miniature brook now runs through a paradise of heathers, rhododendrons and water plants: primulas, kalmia, pieris, enkianthus and meconopsis, with great clumps of cultivated meadow-sweet (spirea). This imaginative posing of exotics among the gigantic timber of the ancient plantation makes a fairyland which calls for a performance of *A Midsummer Night's Dream*, where Titania might ill-meet her Oberon, or whisper her folly in Bottom's furry ear. This spot is a thousand miles from the Industrial Age and the twentieth century. I fear to praise it further, for its beauty is still contained in its silences and its seclusion. But it is surely one of the most beautiful retreats which man, in love with nature, has established in this country, indeed in Europe.

Enthusiasm, however, does not remain in Isabella Plantation, and I am glad to wander away from statistical information, to rove the Park once more with that duty done, free to savour the magic of the place. There are, for instance, the primaeval oaks, survivors of the great Royal forests which once surrounded London. On the north-east, Essex was mainly a forest during the Middle Ages, and the whole of the Kentish and Surrey Weald consisted of the Forest of Anderida, mostly native oaks. They disappeared as the needs of a growing human community called for fuel and timber. Henry VIII and Charles I, devoted to hunting, fortunately preserved certain chases, of which Richmond Park is, with Epping Forest to the east of London, a representative sample of this ancient forest land: English scenery as it was known

The terrace, Pembroke Lodge

to our ancestors, the Saxons, and the Romans and Britons before that. Some of the oaks in Richmond Park must be the oldest in the country, and their mighty trunks, gnarled boles, spreading limbs, wear still the invisible vestments of druidical worship. They have stood there for many centuries, a background to the furious drama of English history. They survive today as a silent commentary on that struggle and that growth, demanding our reverence, if we have any historical imagination by which to recognize the basic character of our country and its people.

I have described the views within the Park. There remains something to be said about that looking out from the Park boundary at the high place just inside Richmond Gate, approaching Pembroke Lodge (now a restaurant where one may enjoy meals in a setting overlooking this wonderful view). To the north-east London and the dome of St. Paul's Cathedral may be seen through an open ride in Sidmouth Wood. A charming iris-garden has been planted on the site of a former house (where possibly the poet Thomson lived) near the gate. It makes a nice contrast in formality with panorama, the view being seen through the gaps in the trees down the terrace garden, with Petersham Park (long incorporated in Richmond) and Ham Common lying below as foreground to the scene. Through the near centre of the picture winds the Thames, coming down from Windsor, whose Castle we can see in the distance. The new buildings of London Airport lie somewhat to the right, and are not unpleasing. There are so many landmarks, however, steeples, mansions, villages, that the eye is unable to command them all, or the mind to appreciate what they signify as they contribute to the wealth of the scene. Farther along the ridge a keeper's lodge was built in the seventeenth or early eighteenth century, later enlarged into a residence; its most interesting feature was the ice-house, surmounted by a summer-house—the Thatched House from which the present Lodge takes its name. The summer-house still survives, decorated with a series of paintings in the style of Angelica Kaufmann.

That sense of height dominates the Park, even though one is wandering in the enclosures, among thickets of green growth. White Lodge, in the middle of the Park, which belonged to the Teck family, and was therefore a home for the late Queen Mary, and beloved by her, is now occupied by the Royal Ballet School.

The panorama from this small Palace has already been described, but it is so dignified, so significant of a way of life that has already vanished, that we can return to it again and again with a mood of nostalgia, if we value tradition, and a structure of society which is giving place to new forms.

We can stand in front of White Lodge and contemplate not only what lies before and around us, but the whole of our exploration of the Royal Parks of London, as we prepare to visit the farthest on our circuit, Hampton Court and Bushy. It is a useful pause, so necessary after the riches, still not wholly absorbed, that began at the gates of Buckingham Palace. Richmond Park is a great repository of history, and especially Royal history, the tale of our kings and queens, and the part they have played in the growth of our democratic way of life, a way which works because of the things shared between all the people; the rights, privileges, and constitutional pleasures, such as these Royal Parks so substantially represent. Down by the warren in Petersham Park, we may look up at the natural ramparts of the Richmond slopes to the great Park which we have just explored. It is a proud and noble enclosure, as we see it from below. The ground slopes gradually across the Petersham flats, then rises steeply, still set with fine timber. The beautiful gardens of Pembroke Lodge (the only formal gardens in the whole of Richmond Park) stand above, and we know what lies beyond, out of sight because of its height; the wild and still sovereign domain that for so many years has been shared with the people, carefully tended, used with respect, an inheritance to be handed on to future generations as a survival of the England where our ancestors inhabited, shaping its character, punctuating its wildness with towns, villages, cathedrals and mansions, various in style, but having in common that Englishness which is so difficult to define, but which we recognize instantly, when we enter the gates of Richmond Park at any point.

Children play on a fallen tree stump

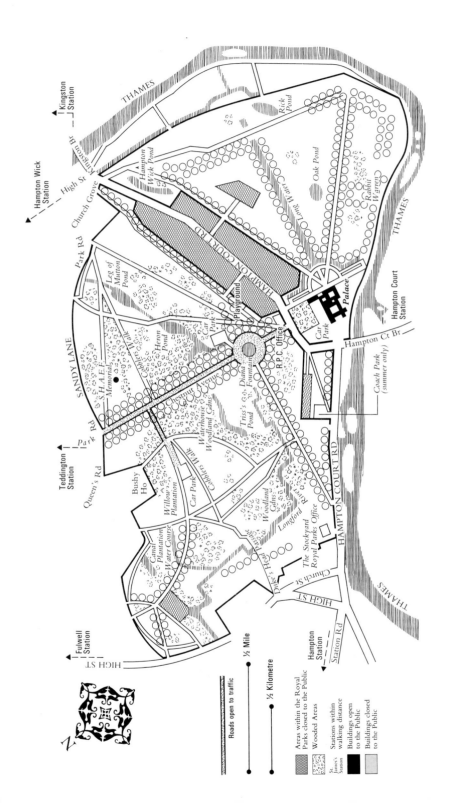

Bushy Park &
Hampton Court

Bushy Park and Hampton Court have to be considered together because they form a huge half-circular unit, with the Thames as diameter and part of the circumference. Each enhances the character of the other. For there is a distinction. Hampton Court Park is the adjunct to a great Palace, and is formally designed to contribute to its stateliness. Bushy has more of the nature of a home farm, and indeed in parts of it one might be deceived into thinking that London was two hundred miles away, beyond the high hedgerows, the tiny streams and foot-bridges, the meadow gates and the sound of the farm machinery at work.

Through the middle of Bushy Park, however, runs the famous chestnut avenue, between the north gate of Hampton Court and Teddington (near the National Physical Laboratory). The Park is large enough (1,099 acres) to absorb this touch of regal formality without being wholly characterized by it. The visitor can walk or ride along the avenue, which is a mile in length, and be sufficiently impressed by the spaciousness of it, admiring the grandure of the ranks of trees each side of the ride, pausing at the Diana fountain to look along the lime avenue that runs off westward into what appears to be wild country past the Waterhouse Plantation, out to Hampton Gate. The popular time to see the chestnut avenue is in spring when the trees are in bloom, the millions of waxen-looking candles serving to remind us of, and to offer tribute to, the genius of Sir Christopher Wren, who laid out the avenue at the time he added the East Court to Hampton Court Palace, in the reign of William III. He intended this avenue to be a ride into a new and classical entrance to the Palace on the north side, but this scheme was not fulfilled, and the avenue ended at the Hampton Court Road and the gate by the Wilderness, the Garden which we shall explore when we enter Hampton Court grounds after leaving Bushy.

Wren also designed the Diana fountain and pond, with the lime avenues to east and west that run from it. The Diana statue, above the fountain, formerly stood in the Privy Garden of the Palace, and was placed in its present position in 1714. The eastern lime avenue peters out, having been truncated in order not to

The Diana Fountain

break into the paddocks, which are used by the Master of the Horse, who is in charge of the Royal Stud Farm.

The half of Bushy Park lying east of the chestnut avenue is the part most used by the public. Just north of the paddocks are a children's playground and pavilion. Several stretches of shallow lake water lie north of these recreation grounds, artificially joined from an outrider of the Longford River, a watercourse cut by Charles I to supply water from the Colne to Hampton Court and the Parks. This was a remarkable piece of engineering, for the river has a completely natural appearance, and adds much to the placid beauty of the lower levels of the Park. Its waters still flow gently, if expensively through the meadows and open ground, tumbling over a waterfall at the entrance to Waterhouse Plantation, feeding the Diana fountain, and the ponds above the paddocks, where a paddling pool for the children has been laid, near their playground.

It also passes through a culvert underneath the road to feed the canal in Hampton Court Gardens and the Long Water in Hampton Court Park, before joining the Thames.

North-east of the artificial ponds (the Heron, and the Leg of Mutton) a large enclosure was sealed off during the war by the American forces. Continuing our travels, we come to the north end of the chestnut avenue at Teddington Gate, thus reaching the wilder half of the Park. We also pass the Park front of Bushy House, a handsome dwelling built by Lord Halifax in the eighteenth century. It was formerly occupied by the Rangers of the Park, amongst whom was William IV while Duke of Clarence. It is now part of the National Physical Laboratory and houses the Director. The Wilderness to the south of it is open to the public, and we can cross this ground while admiring the Georgian façade of the house.

Before us now lies open country, with several plantations to give added character to the scene. The only other enclosure is that of Upper Lodge, built by Charles II, which is now occupied by the Admiralty Research Laboratory.

Turning south we trace the course of the Longford River along the wilder outskirts of the Park, noticing, however, the careful work done since the war in the re-fencing of the boundaries and the plantations. It is here that one has the sensation of being lost in the country, some sleepy lowland where nothing happens except the rotation of the seasons and the agricultural round.

Thus we come to the Waterhouse Plantation, to have our bucollic somnolence broken by surprise; the surprise of a sudden confrontation with unexpected beauty. It is a similar experience to that which we had in the Isabella Plantation in Richmond Park; the realising that here a woodland scene, long matured, has been adapted by an imaginative planning, with a watercourse as the central theme. The sylvan garden here is larger and wilder than that in Richmond Park, and it has vistas of rising and falling glades, culminating in the waterfall of the Longford River. I will not spoil the visitor's pleasure by attempting to describe this delightful place, with its secretive turns and twists, its patterns of contrasted timber and flowering shrub; but I must pay a tribute to the skill with which it has been created. Here and in the Isabella Plantation in

Richmond Park, are two of the most beautiful man-made scenes that I have found anywhere in Europe.

Leaving this pleasance, we walk back along the lime avenue, past the deer-pen, to the Diana fountain, and thence down to the Hampton Court Gate and the approach to the Palace, and its entirely different surroundings. We shall probably have seen the fallow and red deer of Bushy during this part of our wanderings, for they favour this tree-studded ground, which gives them both shade and grazing.

Hampton Court is a world apart, and I hardly know how to sort out the riches and variety of the Palace, the Palace Garden, and the Park. The Palace has a literature to itself, and an official guidebook which can be consulted. We are intent here to explore outside the Palace, and we begin with its immediate environs, the Gardens and the Wilderness, the latter being near at hand as we leave Bushy Park. But by walking round to the green in front of the Palace (a large area of lawns like a village green) we catch the right mood of what may be called historical respect and even reverence, as we wander through the courts of the Palace out to the east front, having duly admired those two interior Gardens, the one Tudor, the other Baroque in setting.

We emerge from the semi-twilight of the courts and corridors of the Palace, to the east front and Fountain Garden, where we must start our exploration before we become too exhausted with sightseeing. Here is formal gardening on a grand scale. In front of the Palace runs the Broad Walk, from the Flowerpot Gates at the top, down past the Wilderness whose ancient wall makes a background to the first great herbaceous border, past the Tudor gardens, almost to the banks of the Thames; nearly half a mile in all, with herbaceous beds stretching the whole length, except for the interruption of Wren's façade to the Palace. The glory of this, its pride of colour and expanse, is something never to forget.

The herbaceous borders face the broad pathway and the parallel runs of lawn, whose immediate punctuation of flower-beds has given the Superintendent an opportunity to display a noble collection of lilies, so appropriate for a riverside garden. This specialization has been carried further in the Wilderness, where a cool dell, set with primulas and lilies, echoes, in miniature, the imaginative harmony of planning done in the Waterhouse Plantation.

Beyond these huge flower-beds and the long stretches of immaculate lawn, the Garden is continued on a plan of fan-shaped paths, set round three extended avenues, the centre of which is the Long Water, stretching down to the low-lying ground within a bend of the Thames. The southern avenue crosses an eighteen-hole golf course. At the Palace end of these avenues, a semicircular canal feeds the Long Water, and between this and the Garden runs a lime-walk, whose ancient trees were planted at the beginning of the eighteenth century.

Even the Park beyond the Gardens is dominated by the personality of the Palace, and as one moves about among the glades, at the river end of the Park, exploring unfrequented corners, discovering such unusual survivals as the old ice-house, the stud house, and other accessories to the Tudor way of life, glimpses of the rose-red Palace intrude, unifying the significance of all this manifest of vanished history.

Gradually this attraction draws us back to the vicinity of the Palace, and having walked up the modern avenue we reach the top of the Garden, which we cross to enter the Privy Garden on the south and Tudor side of the Palace, which Queen Victoria opened to the public in 1894. It is laid out formally, with statues and a fountain, and is bordered by a raised terrace. Queen Mary, wife of William III, reared tropical plants in the greenhouses here, and the alley of pleached wych elm at the west side of the Garden, along the wall, is still called Queen Mary's Bower. The Tijou Screen, at the far end of the Privy Garden, consists of a set of twelve wrought iron panels, designed late in the seventeenth century, by the French metal-smith Jean Tijou. The little Orchard Garden beyond them is reserved for residents in the Palace. The Wren building between that Garden and the Thames is the carefully proportioned banqueting hall built by William III.

The small Knot Garden, in an angle formed by the roseate Tudor brickwork of the Palace walls, was designed in 1924 to illustrate the type of garden fashionable at the end of the sixteenth century. It is thus consonant with the lovely Pond Garden, probably of an origin even earlier than Tudor. Here, with the reconstructed Herb Garden adjoining it, is an example of garden formality at its best, more elaborate even than the Sunken Garden at Kensington Palace which we have already admired. The scent of the box borders, among the most evocative of all garden smells, brings the ghosts of lost summers, year after year, century beyond century, and our drowsing senses conjure back the figures who once walked here, among these diminutive paths: Wolsey, Henry VIII, the ill-fated Charles I, the ladies and the courtiers, most of them, probably, too intent upon the anxieties of Government and the manipulations of office, to be able to enjoy these gardens with the freedom of mind and mood which is our public privilege today.

The Lower Orangery opposite the Herb Garden was built for Queen Anne by Wren, and is an untimely excrescence upon the pure Tudor south façade of the Palace. It used to contain the famous Mantegna Cartoons depicting the Triumph of Caesar, which Charles I, a keen collector of pictures and patron of the arts, bought and placed here.

Having inspected the Orangery, we return to the end of the Privy Garden to see the world-famous Great Vine, which stands in its house close to the Thames. It was planted here in 1769 and is probably the oldest vine in the country. Its bole is eighty-one inches round and the main branch is 114 feet long. It is a *Black Hambro*, a good eating grape, and the fruit is sold to the public at market prices in August. It once bore 2,200 bunches a year at 1 to $1\frac{1}{2}$ lb. a bunch, but it now yields around 650 bunches. The glass screen has been put up to keep off the dust raised by the traffic of visitors.

The return walk through the Privy Garden is welcome because the intimate beauties of the place are revealed only by repeated visits. We make our way now to the north side of the Palace, to enjoy the Wilderness, and the long vista through it right down the entrance to Bushy Park and along the chestnut avenue, a view comparable to the glades of Fontainebleau. The dell, with its primulas and lilies, is at its best in late spring, when the grass beneath the trees in the Wilderness is rich with its full currency of daffodils. The curious Close Tennis Court built by Henry VIII and altered by Charles II adjoins the Broad Walk; and near the Lion Gates will be found the ever-popular maze, planted in the reign of Queen Anne. The close-clipped hedges which line its paths are six feet high and two feet thick.

A woodland pool

During this long exploration, the rose-lover will have been wondering what provision has been made at Hampton Court for his particular enthusiasm. He will be satisfied now that we approach the old Tilt Yard, which lies beside the former Cavalry Barracks in front of the Palace. Henry VIII, who in his early years was an athlete, loved jousting, and wherever he lived he established a Tilt Yard where tournaments were held. William III, who dealt in actual rather than mimic warfare, converted this Tilt Yard into a kitchen garden and subsequently it became a nursery. It now contains a car park, six hard tennis courts, a tea-house and cafeteria, and, most attractive feature, the large rose-garden. This last is well stocked and immaculately kept. It has two plants which I have not seen elsewhere: a gooseberry bush rose and a fruit-bearing pomegranate tree, growing against the north wall.

It is not fanciful to end this tour of the Royal Parks of London with this pointed reference to a pomegranate tree, for we may accept it as a symbol of the rare ingredient of Royalty contained within our democratic community, seasoning it and pronouncing its flavour. These Royal Parks are a facet of that community, an expression of something possessed in pride and maintained in mutuality. They show our English tradition as a living body, flowering here and now, with roots set firmly in our past.

Bibliography

Ashton, J. *Hyde Park from Domesday-Book to date*. London, 1896.

Cecil, Hon. Mrs. E. *London Parks and Gardens*. London, 1907.

Collenette, C. L. *A History of Richmond Park with an Account of its Birds and Animals*. London, 1937.

Dancy, E. *Hyde Park*. London, 1937.

Larwood, J. *The Story of the London Parks*. London, c. 1825.

Law, E. *The History of Hampton Court Palace, vols. 1–3*. London, 1885–91.

Lindsay, P. *Hampton Court: A History*. London, 1948.

Tweedie, Mrs. A. *Hyde Park: its History and Romance*. London, 1908.

Webster, A. D. *Greenwich Park: its History and Associations*. London, 1902.

Webster, A. D. *The Regent's Park and Primrose Hill: History and Antiquities*. London, 1911.

Yates, E. *Hampton Court*. London, 1935.

Reports of the Committee on Bird Sanctuaries in the Royal Parks (England and Wales) for 1928 onwards, published by H.M. Stationery Office for the Ministry of Public Building and Works and now entitled *Bird Life in the Royal Parks*.

Works referred to in the text:

Chesterfield, Lord. *Letters to his Son*. London, 1924.

Cook, Eliza. *Poetical Works*. London, 1870.

Hudson, W. H. *Birds in London*. London, 1898.

Hudson, W. H. *Green Mansions*. London, 1904.

Hudson, W. H. *A Hind in Richmond Park*. London, 1922.

Thomson, James. *The Seasons*. London, 1730.

Wycherley, W. *Love in a Wood, or St. James's Park*. London, 1672.

Time Marches On . . .

It would be remiss if some of the changes that have occurred since Richard Church's book was last issued were not recorded in this edition.

The **Royal Parks** are currently managed by an Agency answerable to the Secretary of State for National Heritage. The position of Chief Executive of the Royal Parks absorbs the role of the former Bailiff, while the Park Superintendents are now known as Park Managers in recognition of their increased responsibilities and range of duties. These include the management of private contractors who carry out the grounds maintenance works previously undertaken by directly employed staff. The Royal Parks also has its own dedicated police force – the Royal Parks Constabulary – which patrols all the Royal Parks – increasingly on horseback. It performs those services which previously fell to park-keepers and (until 1993) to the Metropolitan Police in Hyde Park. The features and amenities of the parks have altered little over the years but some changes have occurred: –

The Serpentine restaurant in **Hyde Park,** a concrete structure redolent of 1960's fashion, was demolished in 1990 and has not been replaced. The park boundary has been more clearly defined by the Queen Elizabeth Gate across South Carriage Drive, near Hyde Park Corner. This new formal entrance to Hyde Park was funded by a trust in honour of Queen Elizabeth, the Queen Mother, and formally opened by Her Majesty the Queen in 1993. On a lesser scale a new manege was constructed adjacent to Rotten Row in 1988 while the generosity of the Sultan of Brunei enabled a riding track to be provided parallel to Park Lane, thus completing a circular rise around Hyde Park. In 1990 the Rotten Row Tercentenary appeal funded the replacement of the cast iron bollards and gas lamps removed for war scrap some 50 years earlier. Few changes have occurred in **St. James's Park** and **Green Park** although present plans include a scheme of floodlighting.

In **The Regent's Park** a new water cascade has brought added delight to Queen Mary's Garden while the Avenue Gardens in the Broad Walk are being restored to the Victorian flamboyance of William Andrews Nesfield's design. New initiatives include the creation of an information and educational centre and one to establish the park as the focus for the welfare and rearing of waterfowl for all the Royal Parks.

The Queen Elizabeth Oak in **Greenwich Park** sadly fell in 1991 after the second of the Great Storms that ravaged so much of the country in 1987 and 1990 but its trunk remains on display alongside a replacement oak tree planted by His Royal Highness Prince Philip, Duke of Edinburgh in 1992. Rangers House is now owned and managed by English Heritage as successors to London County Council (and later the Greater London Council) while the operational headquarters of the Royal Observatory have moved again from Sussex to Cambridge. The Herb Garden alongside St. Mary's Gate has been restored while future plans include a new interpretation centre, the re-development of the former nursery site and the re-instatement of the escarpments and Le Notre's Giant Steps.

Richmond Park now enjoys the added protection following its designation as a Special Site of Scientific Interest (SSSI) and current management initiatives are being directed towards the conservation and encouragement of a wide variety of wildlife (from beetles to badgers!) The park has also recently seen the re-introduction of the heavy working horse and now boasts two shires to help with traditional land management.

Similar policies are being pursued in **Bushy Park** and a new wildlife educational centre is being established in the former storeyard for the benefit of adults and schoolchildren alike.

The Royal Parks
August 1993